Collins Complete Wiring and Lighting

Collins

complete

wiring AND

lighting

Albert Jackson and David Day

Collins

Collins Complete Wiring and Lighting
was originally created for HarperCollins Publishers by
Inklink/Jackson Day Jennings. Most of the material in
this book also appears in *Collins Complete DIY Manual*.

This new edition first published in 2008 by
Collins, an imprint of
HarperCollinsPublishers
77-85 Fulham Palace Road
Hammersmith
London W6 8JB

Collins is a registered trademark
of HarperCollins Publishers Ltd

13   12   11   10   09   08
6   5   4   3   2   1

A catalogue record for this book is available from
The British Library

ISBN 978 000 726728 6

Colour reproduction by Colourscan, Singapore
Printed and bound by Printing Express, Hong Kong

PLEASE NOTE
**Great care has been taken to ensure that the
information contained in Collins Complete Wiring and
Lighting is accurate. However, the law concerning
Building Regulations, planning, local bylaws and
related matters is neither static nor simple. A book
of this nature cannot replace specialist advice in
appropriate cases and therefore no responsibility
can be accepted by the publishers or by the authors
for any loss or damage caused by reliance upon the
accuracy of such information.**

**If you live outside Britain, your local conditions
may mean that some of this information is not
appropriate. If in doubt, always consult a qualified
electrician, plumber or surveyor.**

Authors
Albert Jackson and David Day

Photographers
Colin Bowling
Paul Chave
Ben Jennings
Neil Waving

Consultant
John Dees

Design
Elizabeth Standley

New Illustrations
Graham White

Illustrations
Robin Harris
John Pinder

Editors
Peter Leek
Barbara Dixon

Proofreader and Indexer
Mary Morton

Acknowledgements
The authors and publishers would like to thank the following
companies and individuals who supplied images or tools for
photography:

7 DEFRA; 43 Graham Dixon; 46 Ikea; 50 Ikea, Ring Lighting;
58 Ikea; 65 Oase Living Water, Rodney Hyett/Elizabeth
Whiting Associates; 69 Jewson, Irwin Tools, Screwfix

Contents

Electricity

Reducing electricity bills

Pressures from all sides urge us to conserve energy. But even without such encouragement, our electricity bills would provide stimulus enough to make us find ways of using less power. Nobody wants to live in a poorly heated or dismally lit house without the comforts of hot water, refrigeration and other conveniences – but it is possible to identify where energy is wasted and find ways to reduce waste without compromising comfort or pleasure.

Fitting controls to save money

As the chart opposite clearly shows, heating is by far the biggest consumer of domestic power. One way to reduce your electricity bills is to fit devices that regulate the heating in your home to suit your lifestyle, maintaining comfortable but economic temperatures.

Thermostats

Most modern heating has some form of thermostatic control – a device that will switch power off when surroundings reach a certain temperature. Many thermostats are marked out simply to increase or decrease the temperature, in which case you have to experiment with various settings to find the one that suits you best. If the thermostat settings are more precise, try 18°C (65°F) for everyday use – although elderly people are more comfortable at about 21°C (70°F).

As well as saving you money, an immersion-heater thermostat prevents your water from becoming dangerously hot. Set it at 60°C (140°F). See right for Economy 7 settings.

Time switches

Even when it's thermostatically controlled, heating is expensive if run continuously – but you can install an automatic time switch to turn it on and off at preset times, so you get up in the morning and arrive home in the evening to a warm house. Set it to turn off the heating about half an hour before you leave home or go to bed, as the house will take time to cool down.

A similar device will ensure that your water is at its hottest when needed.

● **Insulation**
Measures taken to save energy will have little effect unless you insulate your house as well as the hot-water cylinder and pipework. You can do most of the work yourself for a relatively modest outlay and a little effort.

Off-peak rates

Electricity is normally sold at a general-purpose rate, every unit used costing the same; but if you warm your home with storage heaters and heat your water electrically, then you can take advantage of the economical off-peak tariff. This system, called Economy 7, allows you to charge storage heaters and heat water at less than half the general-purpose rate for seven hours, starting between midnight and 1 a.m. Other appliances used during that time get cheap power too, so more savings can be made by running the dishwasher or washing machine after you've gone to bed. Each appliance must, of course, be fitted with a timer. The Economy 7 daytime rate is higher than the general-purpose one, but the cost of running 24-hour appliances such as freezers and refrigerators is balanced since they also use cheap power for seven hours.

For full benefit from off-peak water heating, use a cylinder that holds 182 to 227 litres (40 to 50 gallons), to store as much cheap hot water as possible. You will need a twin-element heater or two separate units. One heater, near the base of the cylinder, heats the whole tank on cheap power; another, about half way up, tops up the hot water during the day. Set the night-time heater at 75°C (167°F), the daytime one at 60°C (140°F).

The electricity companies provide Economy 7 customers with a special meter to record daytime and night-time consumption separately, plus a timer that automatically switches the supply from one rate to the other.

Monitoring consumption

Keep an accurate record of your energy saving by taking weekly readings. Note the dates of any measures taken to cut power consumption, and compare the corresponding drop in meter readings.

Digital meters

Modern meters display a row of digits that represent the total number of units consumed since the meter was installed. To calculate the number of units used since your last electricity bill, simply subtract the 'present reading' shown on your bill from the number of units now shown on the meter. Make sure that the bill gives an actual reading and not an estimate (indicated by the letter 'E' before the reading).

Reading dial meters

Older installations may incorporate a meter with a set of dials that indicate the consumption of electricity. With a bit of practice you will be able to read these meters yourself. Ignore the dial marked ¹⁄₁₀, which is only for testing. Start with the dial indicating single units (kWh) and, working from right to left, record the readings from the 10, 100, 1000 and finally 10,000 unit dials. Note the digits the pointers have passed. If a pointer is, say, between 5 and 6, record 5. If it's right on a number, say 8, check the next dial on the right: if that pointer is between 9 and 0, record 7; if it's past 0, record 8. Also, remember that adjacent dials revolve in opposite directions, alternating along the row.

Digital meter display

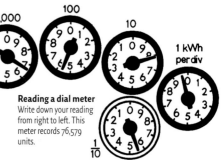

Reading a dial meter
Write down your reading from right to left. This meter records 76,579 units.

SEE ALSO > Immersion heaters 40–1

Lower running costs

In Britain there are now more than twenty companies who supply electricity and gas – which means that shopping around may help you find a better deal. Supply companies play no part in the actual generation and distribution of electricity and gas, even if their parent company is involved with these activities. Whichever supplier you go with, the responsibility for meters and incoming cables and pipes remains unchanged.

Buying your energy at the lowest price

The tariffs offered by all the energy-supply companies are a combination of a standing charge and unit costs for the energy supplied. Unit costs vary, depending on whether the energy is supplied during the day or at night, and block charges for consumption above a certain level may reduce unit costs still further. In addition, discounts are usually available if you adopt methods of payment such as direct debit that are more convenient for the supply companies. There is also some incentive to choose a company who can supply both electricity and gas. Every company seeks to make its tariffs seem more attractive than those of its competitors – but the only figure that is important to you, the customer, is the total you pay each year for your energy.

Comparing prices

The government website **www.energywatch.org.uk** provides a code to be followed by price-comparison websites. Examples of websites that adhere to this code are **www.energylinx.co.uk**, **www.which.co.uk** and **www.uSwitch.com** These sites will supply you with estimates of costs from each supplier and compare those against your present outgoings. Make sure you don't log on to a website created on behalf of one particular supplier. Once

you have made the choice to switch to another supplier, it is often possible to make the transfer on-line.

You can use the same 'comparison' sites to check on how easy it is to make a transfer to a potential supplier and find out what policies they have in relation to environmentally sensitive issues.

To carry out a meaningful comparison you will need to supply:
• Your postcode
• Your present suppliers of gas and electricity
• The type of meter (normal or Economy 7)
• Your annual consumption of each fuel or your present annual bills.
• The units used at night (for Economy 7 customers) expressed as either a number of units or a percentage of the total units

Though most companies offer discounts for customers who take both gas and electricity from the same supplier, you may find that it is more economical to purchase each fuel separately. Try entering the same details for gas and electricity only and compare the results with a quote for a combined tariff.

Within the constraints imposed by the government watchdog, energy suppliers are continually adjusting their prices, and it may be worth comparing costs at about the same time each year.

Energy-efficiency labelling

When you're shopping for new appliances, look for the European Community Energy Label that must by law be available at the point of sale, including web sites on the internet. This labelling gives guidance on energy efficiency for electrical equipment from light bulbs to dishwashers, and the choice of an 'A' rating can make considerable savings in running costs.

European flower
Any appliance bearing this symbol will be the best in its class in terms of all environmental criteria.

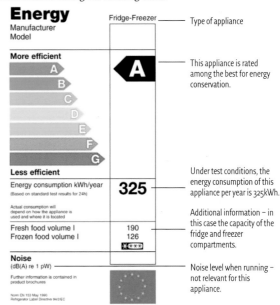

Type of appliance

This appliance is rated among the best for energy conservation.

Under test conditions, the energy consumption of this appliance per year is 325kWh.

Additional information – in this case the capacity of the fridge and freezer compartments.

Noise level when running – not relevant for this appliance.

Typical running costs

Apart from the standing charge, your electricity bill is based on the number of units of electricity you have consumed during a given period. Each unit represents the amount used in one hour by a 1kW appliance. An appliance rated at 3kW will use the same amount of energy in 20 minutes. To help you identify the heavy users of energy, the chart on the right groups typical appliances under headings for low, medium and high electricity consumption.

LOW ENERGY CONSUMERS Less than 100 units per year	MEDIUM ENERGY CONSUMERS 100 to 1000 units per year	HIGH ENERGY CONSUMERS More than 1000 units per year
Toasters	Refrigerators	Instant water heaters
Coffee percolators	Freezers	Dishwashers
Slow cookers	Cookers	Immersion water heaters
Cooker hoods	Electric kettles	Fan heaters
Microwave ovens	Extractor fans	Electric fires
VCRs and DVD players	Washing machines	Whole-house lighting using GLS lamps (ordinary bulbs)
Stereo systems	Tumble dryers	Whole-house electric heating
Electric blankets	Irons	
Shavers	Vacuum cleaners	
Hairdryers	Colour TVs	
Power tools	Compact fluorescent house lighting	
Hedge trimmers	Instant showers	
Lawn mowers	Heated towel rails	

SEE ALSO > Heating water 40–1, Comparing bulbs and tubes 51

First things first

Before you undertake any electrical work, familiarize yourself with the basic facts on how a domestic system works and make sure you understand how to proceed safely. You also need to be aware of the current regulations that cover electrical wiring in the home.

Understanding the basics

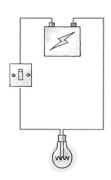

A basic circuit
Electricity runs from the source (battery) to the appliance (bulb) and then returns to the source. A switch breaks the circuit to interrupt the flow of electricity.

Electrical circuits are based on simple principles. For any electrical appliance to work, the power must be able to flow along a wire from its source to the appliance (say, a light bulb) and then back to the source along another wire. If the circuit is broken at any point, the appliance will stop working – the bulb will go out. Breaking the circuit – and restoring it as required – is what a switch is for. When the switch is in the 'on' position, the circuit is complete and the bulb operates. Turning the switch off makes a gap in the circuit, so the electricity stops flowing.

Mains electricity in your home flows through live or 'phase' wires linked to every light, socket outlet and fixed electrical appliance in your home. The current flows back out of the building through the neutral wires.

Earthing

Any material through which electricity can flow is known as a conductor. Most metals conduct electricity well, which is why copper is used for electrical wiring. The earth itself – the ground on which we stand – is also an extremely good conductor, which is why electricity always flows into the earth whenever it can, taking the shortest available route. This means that if you were to touch a live conductor, the current would divert and take the short route to the earth – through your body.

A similar thing can happen if a live wire accidentally comes into contact with any exposed metal component of an appliance, including its casing. To prevent this, a third wire is included in the system and connected to the earth, usually via the outer casing of the electricity company's main service cable. This third wire – called the earth wire – is attached to the metal casing of some appliances and to earth terminals in others, providing a direct route to the ground should a fault occur. This sudden change of route by the electricity – known as an earth fault – causes a fuse to blow or circuit breaker to operate, cutting off the current.

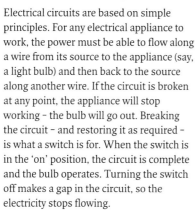

Measuring electricity

Watts measure the amount of power used by an appliance when working. The wattage of an electrical appliance is normally marked on its casing. One thousand watts (1000W) equal one kilowatt (1kW).

Amps measure the flow of current that is necessary to produce the required wattage for an appliance.

Volts measure the 'pressure' provided by the electricity company. This drives the current along the conductors to the various outlets. In this country 230 volts (formerly 240) is standard.

If you know two of these measurements, you can determine the other one.

$\dfrac{\text{Watts}}{\text{Volts}} = \text{Amps}$	Amps x Volts = Watts
Use this method to determine what kind of fuse or flex is safe.	Indicates how much power is needed to operate an appliance.

Double insulation
Appliances that are double-insulated – which usually means they have a plastic casing that insulates the user from metal parts that could become live – must not be earthed with a third wire. A square within a square, either printed or moulded on an appliance, means it is double-insulated and its flex does not need an earth wire.

N

Notifiable work
To help you decide which electrical work you can do yourself, all notifiable work shown in this book is marked with this symbol.

Building Regulations on electrical wiring

Regulations – known as Part P of the Building Regulations – have been introduced to promote better standards. Similar legislation for Scotland is covered by the Building Standards (Scotland) Regulations. These regulations do not prevent the DIY worker from undertaking electrical wiring, but they put strict limits on what can be done without supervision and inspection.

All local authorities have Building Control Officers (BCOs) who are responsible for monitoring the regulations. You should therefore contact your BCO to ascertain how exactly your particular authority applies the regulations.

Certain tasks can be undertaken without having to notify the authority, and most BCOs do not require any communication or paperwork for 'non-notifiable' electrical work. However, where similar work is carried out in locations such as kitchens and bathrooms or the wiring will be complicated or extensive, then the work becomes 'notifiable' and must be discussed with the BCO before it is carried out.

Non-notifiable work

A DIY worker can do the following, anywhere in the home without having to inform the BCO in advance:
• Replace sockets, fused connection units, switches and ceiling roses.
• Replace damaged cable for a single circuit.
• Refix or replace enclosures (mounting boxes for sockets and switches) on existing circuits.
• Provide mechanical protection in the form of conduit and plastic channel.

Also without having to inform the BCO in advance, a DIY worker can do the following anywhere in the home except in kitchens, bathrooms and utility rooms and in special locations – such as rooms with a bathtub or shower, swimming pools and paddling pools, hot-air saunas and outdoors – or when installing extra-low-voltage lighting:
• Add new light fittings and switches to existing circuits.
• Add new socket outlets to existing ring circuits and radial circuits.
• Add fused spurs to existing ring circuits and radial circuits.

Notifiable work

The BCO must be notified before a DIY worker undertakes any electrical work not listed above or if the work is categorized as one of the exceptions described above.

Although DIY electricians are permitted to carry out notifiable work, the cost and complexity of obtaining approval, testing, and certification from the BCO (see opposite) may make it more economical to have such work done by a professional electrician.

SEE ALSO > Testing circuits 12–13, Flex 16, Switching off 20, Earthing and bonding 21, Fuses and circuit breakers 23, Cable 26

Complying with the regulations

It is not necessary to involve the BCO when any work is undertaken by a professional electrician – that is a competent person registered with an electrical self-certification scheme. He or she will deal with all the paperwork required by the authority and, on completion of the work, should give you a signed Building Regulations Self-certification Certificate and a completed Electrical Installation Certificate.

If you feel competent to do any notifiable work yourself, you must tell your local BCO in advance exactly what you propose to do. Having obtained permission to proceed, once you have completed the work you must ask the BCO to send an inspector to test the installation and issue a certificate. A fee will be charged for inspection and testing. Most BCOs will offer some concession – such as including the electrical inspection in the general inspection costs for building a new extension. Some BCOs may ask you to arrange for a competent electrician to inspect and test the work.

Procedures are laid down for appeals, determinations, relaxations and dispensations, but the common-sense approach is to accept any advice or instruction given by your local Building Control Officer.

Provided you are competent to undertake non-notifiable work, you may proceed without supervision so long as the methods used comply with the the IEE Wiring Regulations (BS7671). Good workmanship and the use of proper materials are fundamental to these regulations. You should also keep a record of your work in the form of a Minor Electrical Works Certificate, which you can pass on to interested parties should you decide to sell your home in the future. Selling a house without appropriate paperwork may introduce delays and difficulties.

The methods and materials suggested in this book comply with the Wiring Regulations, but you should be aware that the rigorous final testing of installations, which has to be carried out by qualified persons using specialized equipment, falls outside the scope of this book. If you have any doubts about your ability to satisfy the requirements of the Wiring Regulations, then use this book to study the work involved so you can brief a professional electrician and agree an appropriate price for the job. Ensure that any electrician you hire is a member of an authorized competent-person self-certification scheme.

With safety in mind

Throughout this chapter you will find frequent references to the need for safety while working on your electrical system – but it cannot be stressed too strongly that you must also take steps to safeguard yourself and anyone else using the system. Faulty wiring and appliances are dangerous, and can be lethal.

- Never inspect or work on any part of an electrical installation without first switching off the power at the consumer unit and removing the relevant circuit fuse or locking off the miniature circuit breaker (MCB).
- Always unplug a portable appliance or light before doing any work on it.
- Always use the correct tools and use good-quality equipment and materials.
- Always double-check all your work (especially connections) before you turn the electricity on again.
- Fuses are vital safety devices. Never fit one that's rated too highly for the circuit it is to protect – and never be tempted to use any other type of wire or metal strip in place of proper fuses or fuse wire.
- Wear rubber-soled shoes when you're working on an electrical installation.

Colour coding

For purpose of identification, the coverings of live, neutral and earth wires in flex and mains cables are colour-coded. The live wires are brown and the neutral wires blue.

When an earth wire is included in a piece of flex, it is coded with a green-and-yellow covering. In a mains cable, the earth is a bare copper wire. Whenever the earth wire is exposed for linking to socket outlets or light fittings, it should be covered with a green-and-yellow sleeve.

Until recently the live and neutral wires in mains cables were coded with other colours. Live wires had a red covering, and neutral wires a black covering. There is no reason to replace old colour-coded cables, but whenever you need to join new cable to old, remember to connect the brown wire to the old red one, and the blue wire to the old black one.

Identifying conductors
The insulation used to cover the conductors in electrical cable and flex is colour-coded to indicate live, neutral and earth.

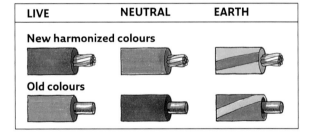

LIVE	NEUTRAL	EARTH
New harmonized colours		
Old colours		

Fuses and circuit breakers

A conductor will heat up if an unusually powerful current flows through it. This can damage electrical equipment and create a serious fire risk if it is allowed to continue. As a safeguard weak links are included in the wiring, to break the circuit before the current reaches a dangerously high level.

Fuses

A very common form of protection is a fuse, a thin wire that's designed to break the circuit by melting at a specific current. This varies according to the part of the system that the fuse is protecting – an individual appliance, a single power or lighting circuit, or the entire domestic wiring system.

Miniature circuit breakers

Alternatively, a special switch called a circuit breaker is used that trips and cuts off the current as soon as an overload on the wiring is detected.

A fuse will 'blow' (or an MCB will trip) in the following circumstances:
- If too many appliances are operated on a circuit simultaneously, then the excessive demand for electricity will blow the fuse in that circuit.
- If the current reroutes to earth due to a faulty appliance, the flow of power increases in the circuit and blows the fuse (this is known as an earth fault).

SEE ALSO > Flex 16, Switching off the power 20, Fuses and circuit breakers 23, Cable 26

Bathroom safety

Because water is such a highly efficient conductor of electric current, water and electricity form a very dangerous combination. For this reason, in terms of electricity, bathrooms are potentially the most dangerous areas in your home. Where there are so many exposed metal pipes and fittings, combined with wet conditions, regulations must be stringently observed if fatal accidents are to be avoided.

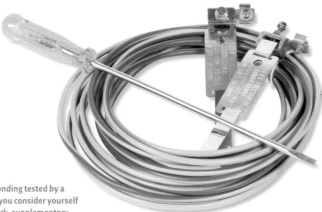

N If you undertake work marked with this symbol, you must inform the BCO before starting – see FIRST THINGS FIRST.

WARNING
Have your supplementary bonding tested by a qualified electrician. Unless you consider yourself fully competent to do the work, supplementary bonding must be installed by a professional.

GENERAL SAFETY

- Sockets must not be fitted in a bathroom – except for special shaver sockets that conform to BS EN 60742 Chapter 2, Section 1.

- The IEE Wiring Regulations stipulate that light switches in bathrooms must be outside zones 0 to 3 (see opposite). The best way to comply with this requirement is to fit ceiling-mounted pull-cord switches.

- When installing an electrical appliance in a bathroom, the relevant circuit should be protected by a 30 milliamp RCD.

- If you have a shower in a bedroom, it must be not less than 3m (9ft 11in) from any socket outlet, which must be protected by a 30 milliamp RCD.

- Light fittings in a bathroom must be well out of reach and shielded – so fit a close-mounted ceiling light, properly enclosed, rather than a pendant fitting.

- Never use a portable appliance, such as a hairdryer, in a bathroom – even if it is plugged into a socket outside the room.

Supplementary bonding **N**

In any bathroom there are many nonelectrical metallic components, such as metal baths and basins, supply pipes to bath and basin taps, metal waste pipes, radiators, central-heating pipework and so on – all of which could cause an accident during the time it would take for an electrical fault to blow a fuse or trip a miniature circuit breaker. To ensure that no dangerous voltages are created between metal parts, all these metal components must be connected one to another by a conductor which is itself connected to a terminal on the earthing block in the consumer unit. This is known as supplementary bonding and is required for all bathrooms – even when there is no electrical equipment installed in the room, and even though the water and gas pipes are bonded to the consumer's earth terminal near the consumer unit.

When electrical equipment, such as a heater or shower, is fitted in a bathroom, that too must be bonded by connecting its metalwork – such as the casing – to the nonelectrical metal pipework.

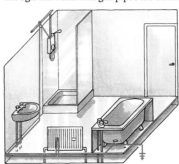

Supplementary bonding in a bathroom

Making the connections

The Wiring Regulations specify the minimum size of earthing conductor that can be used for supplementary bonding in different situations, so that large-scale electrical installations can be costed economically. However, 6mm² single-core cable, insulated with green-and-yellow PVC, is large enough to be safe for supplementary bonding in any domestic situation. For a neat appearance, the route of the bonding cable should be planned to run behind the bath panel, under floorboards, and through basin pedestals. If necessary, the cable can be run through a hollow wall or under plaster.

Connecting to pipework
An earth clamp is used for making connections to pipework. The pipe should be cleaned locally with wire wool to make a good connection between the pipe and clamp. Scrape or strip an area of paintwork if the pipe has been painted.

Attach an earth clamp to the pipework

Connecting to a bath or basin
Metal baths or basins are made with an earth tag. To connect the earth cable, the bared end of the conductor should be trapped under a nut and bolt with metal washers. Make sure the tag has not been painted or enamelled.

If an old metal bath or basin has not been provided with an earth tag, drill a hole through the foot of the bath or through the rim at the back of the basin; so that the cable can be connected with a similar nut and bolt, with metal washers.

Connecting to an appliance
The bonding cable must be connected to the earth terminal provided in the electrical appliance and then run to a clamp on a metal supply pipe nearby.

SEE ALSO > Building Regulations 8, Bonding to earth 20–1, Cable 26, Running cable 27–9, Wiring a shower 40

Zones for bathrooms

Within a room containing a bath or shower, the Wiring Regulations define areas, or zones, where specific safety precautions apply. The regulations also describe what type of appliances can be installed in each zone, and the routes cables must take. There are special considerations for extra-low-voltage equipment with separated earth.

The four zones

Any room containing a bathtub or shower is divided into four zones. Zone 0 is the interior of the bathtub or shower tray – not including the space beneath the tub, which is covered by other regulations (see right). Zones 1 to 3 are specific areas above and around the bath or shower, where only specified electrical appliances and their cables may be installed. Wiring outside these areas must conform to the IEE Wiring Regulations, but no specific 'zone' regulations apply.

ZONE	LOCATION	PERMITTED
Zone 0	Interior of the bathtub or shower tray.	No electrical installation.
Zone 1	Directly above the bathtub or shower tray, up to a height of 2.25m (7ft 5in) from the floor. (See also UNDER THE BATH, right.)	Instantaneous water heater. Instantaneous shower. All-in-one power shower, with a suitably waterproofed integral pump. The wiring that serves appliances within the zone.
Zone 2	Area within 0.6m (2ft) horizontally from the bathtub or shower tray in any direction, up to a height of 2.25m (7ft 5in) from the floor. The area above zone 1, up to a height of 3m (9ft 11in) from the floor.	Appliances permitted in zone 1. Light fittings. Extractor fan. Space heater. Whirlpool unit for the bathtub. Shaver socket to BS EN 60742 Chapter 2, Section 1. The wiring that serves appliances within the zone and any appliances in zone 1.
Zone 3	Up to 2.4m (7ft 11in) outside zone 2, up to a height of 2.25m (7ft 5in) from the floor. The area above zone 2 next to the bathtub or shower, up to a height of 3m (9ft 11in) from the floor.	Appliances permitted in zones 1 and 2. Any fixed electrical appliance (a heated towel rail, for example) that is protected by a 30 milliamp RCD. The wiring that serves appliances within the zone and any appliances in zones 1 and 2.

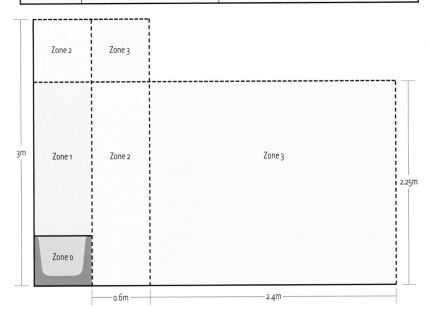

3m
2.25m
0.6m   2.4m

Zones within a room containing a bath or shower

Under the bath

The space under a bathtub is designated as zone 1 if it is accessible without having to use a tool – that is, if there is no bath panel or if the panel is attached with magnetic catches or similar devices that allow the panel to be detached without using a tool of some kind. If, however, the panel is screw-fixed, then the enclosed space beneath the bath is considered to be outside all zones.

Supplementary bonding

In bathrooms, nonelectrical metallic components must be bonded to earth (see opposite). In zones 1, 2 and 3, this bonding is required to all pipes, any electrical appliances and any exposed metallic structural components of the building. This does not include window frames, unless they are themselves connected to metallic structural components.

Supplementary bonding is not required outside the zones. In the case of a shower cubicle in a bedroom, supplementary bonding can also be omitted from zone 3.

- **Cable runs**
You are not permitted to run electrical cables that are feeding a zone through another zone designated with a lower number. This includes cables buried in the plaster or concealed behind other wallcoverings.

Switches

Electrical switches, including ceiling-mounted switches operated by a pull cord, must be situated outside the zones. The only exceptions are those switches and controls incorporated in appliances suitable for use in the zones.

If the bathroom ceiling is higher than 3m (9ft 11in), pull-cord switches can be mounted anywhere. However, if the ceiling height is between 2.25 and 3m (7ft 5in and 9ft 11in), pull-cord switches must be mounted at least 0.6m (2ft) – measured horizontally – from the bathtub or shower cubicle. If the ceiling is lower than 2.25m (7ft 5in), switches must be outside the room.

- **13amp sockets**
In the special case of a bedroom containing a shower cubicle, socket outlets are permitted in the room, but only outside the zones, and the circuit that feeds the sockets must be protected by a 30 milliamp RCD.

IP coding

Electrical appliances installed in zones 1 and 2 must be made with suitable protection against splashed water. This is designated by the code IPX4 (the letter X is sometimes replaced with a single digit). Any number larger than four is also acceptable as this indicates a higher degree of waterproofing. If in doubt, check with your supplier.

IP coding
Suitable equipment may be marked with this symbol.

SEE ALSO > Wiring a shower 40, Light switches 53

Testing circuits

For your own safety and for the safety of others using or working on your electrical installation in the future, carry out the tests recommended here each time you work on the fixed wiring of your home. Although these tests should not be regarded as substitutes for those required by Building Control Officers, if your work passes them it is likely to meet the requirements of the regulations.

Test instruments

Ohms and MegOhms
On some multimeters, Ohms are indicated by the symbol Ω and MegOhms (millions of Ohms) by MΩ.

There are many different testers to choose from, and those at the top end of the market may cost hundreds of pounds. However, reliable testers can be purchased for much less.

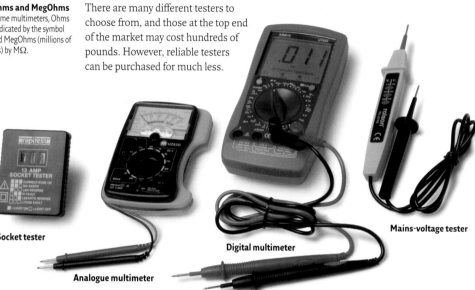

Socket tester

Analogue multimeter

Digital multimeter

Mains-voltage tester

Required testing

Carry out the tests described opposite to check the effectiveness of the fixed wiring of your house. However, the Building Regulations require final testing with specialist equipment, which is used by Building Control inspectors and other professionals to provide readings that can be entered on the necessary certificates.

Is the power off?

Having turned off the power at the consumer unit, make sure an accessory is safe to work on by using an electronic mains-voltage tester to check whether terminals or wires are live, before you tamper with them. Always make sure the tester is functioning properly both before and after you use it, by testing it on a circuit you know to be live.

Following the manufacturer's instructions, place one probe on the neutral terminal and the other on the live terminal; if the indicator lights up, the circuit is live. If it doesn't illuminate, test again – this time between the earth terminal and each of the live and neutral terminals. If the indicator still doesn't light up, you can assume the circuit is not live – provided you have checked the tester.

1 Insulation resistance
Set the selector to the highest resistance scale.

Mains-voltage tester
Mains testers are designed to tell you whether a circuit is completely 'dead' after you have turned off the power at the consumer unit. Be sure to buy a tester that's intended for use with mains voltage – similar devices are sold in auto shops for 12V car wiring only.

Multimeters
There are digital multimeters that give readings on an LCD screen, and there are analogue instruments with a needle that moves across a scale on a dial.

Both types have a rotary selector for setting the meter to measure voltage, current, resistance and other values. When testing insulation resistance and continuity (see opposite), you want the meter to measure resistance. For insulation resistance, set the selector to the highest resistance range (**1**); for continuity, set it to the lowest resistance range (**2**). With some multimeters, you can select an audible signal to tell you when there is continuity.

With an analogue multimeter, a reading at the lower end of the scale indicates a

2 Continuity
Set the selector to the lowest resistance scale.

continuous, unbroken circuit. A reading at the top end of the scale means there is an 'open' circuit – there's a break somewhere on the circuit.

With an analogue meter, satisfactory insulation resistance is indicated when the needle is at the top end of the scale, showing a reading of millions of Ohms (MegOhms).

When using a digital multimeter, for continuity you are looking for a low value – less than 10 Ohms. For satisfactory insulation resistance, you want a value of more than 10 million Ohms (10 MegOhms).

To test that a multimeter is working, touch the two probes together and the meter should read zero. Move the probes apart and it should read infinity. The manufacturers of digital multimeters use the figure 1 (with no other figures after the decimal point) to mean infinity – which simply indicates a very high resistance.

Socket tester
A simple plug-in device can be used to test the connections inside a 13amp socket outlet without having to turn off the power or expose internal wiring.

Using a mains-voltage tester
Touch the neutral terminal with one probe and the live terminal with the other. The circuit is live if the indicator illuminates.

SEE ALSO > Building Regulations 8, Consumer units 22

Protective devices

As part of the testing required by Building Control Officers, an inspector uses equipment that checks whether protective devices (miniature circuit breakers and residual current devices) are operating within the times specified in the regulations. This is a procedure that falls outside the scope of this book.

However, you can at least ensure an RCD trips satisfactorily when you press its test button, and you can test that an MCB is working by operating its switch. Test these devices every time you carry out electrical work on your home, and also at regular intervals – say every three months or so.

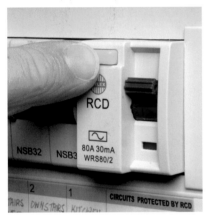

Press the test button on a residual current device

Checking polarity

Having worked on an electrical circuit, before replacing sockets, switches or faceplates, always double-check that the live, neutral and earth conductors are connected to their respective terminals.

Having switched the power back on, you can use a plug-in tester to check the wiring to your socket outlets. Switch on the socket; and if all three indicator lights come on, the socket is wired correctly.

If all three lights come on, polarity is correct

Testing for continuity

In simple terms, a continuity test is designed to check that there is an electrical connection between two points, say between the two ends of a length of wire. This is done with a multimeter set to its lowest resistance range. Place one of the instrument's probes on each end of the wire. A low reading on the dial or screen means the wire is continuous – there is continuity. A high reading means the wire is broken somewhere along its length – so there's no continuity.

You can use this test to check whether a cartridge fuse has blown, or whether a ring circuit is continuous or a heating element is working.

Testing a ring circuit

This is an important test because a ring circuit could still be functioning even when there's a break somewhere on the circuit. At the consumer unit, having first turned off the main switch, identify the two ends of the cable feeding the ring circuit; then remove the live, neutral and earth conductors from their terminals and separate all the wires.

Testing insulation resistance

This test is designed to make sure there is no current leaking through the insulation between two conductors, say live and neutral. If this is allowed to happen there is a danger of overheating – which could cause a fire. Alternatively, there could be a short circuit and the fuse protecting the circuit would blow or the MCB would trip.

You should test any circuit you have worked on. Make sure the power is turned off, then unplug every appliance on the circuit and check that all switches are turned off. This includes switches for all fixed appliances.

At the consumer unit, identify the cable feeding the relevant circuit and disconnect the conductors from their terminals. If you are installing a new circuit, do the test before making the final connections at the consumer unit.

With a multimeter set to its highest resistance range, place one probe on the live (red or brown) conductor and the other probe on the neutral (black or blue) conductor. If the reading shown on the meter is low, the insulation resistance is suspect and should be investigated. If the reading is high – in the order of MegOhms – the insulation resistance is satisfactory. Repeat the test between the live conductor and earth (green-and-yellow) conductor

Testing for continuity
Touch one end of the wire with one probe and the other end of the same wire with the other probe. A low reading (shown above) indicates that the wire is continuous.

Carry out the continuity test between the two ends of the live (red or brown) conductor. Repeat the test on the neutral (black or blue) conductor, and then on the earth (yellow-and-green) conductor. A low reading (low resistance) for each test means there is continuity on all three conductors – each is continuous, which is how it should be.

If you get a high reading, check every socket outlet, junction box and fused connection unit to make sure there are no loose connections and then perform the continuity test again.

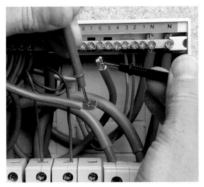

Insulation resistance
Touch the neutral conductor with one probe and the live conductor with the other. A high reading (shown above) indicates satisfactory insulation resistance.

and then between the neutral and earth, looking for a high reading in each case.

Investigating a suspect circuit

With the power turned off, inspect the suspect wiring, including every accessory (socket, switch, junction box and so on), starting with the ones you have been working on. Typical causes of low insulation resistance are:
• A damp wall or water running into an accessory.
• A nail or screw driven through a cable.
• Rodent damage to cables.
• Old rubber-insulated cables connected to the circuit.
• Conductors crushed together by careless replacement of a socket outlet or switch.

SEE ALSO > Building Regulations 8, RCDs 21–2, Consumer units 22, MCBs 23, Resetting an MCB 24, Checking fuses 24, Domestic circuits 25, Adding a spur to a ring 33, Wiring a cooker 38–9, Replacing an element 41

Assessing your installation

Inspect the electrical installation in your home to ensure that it is safe and adequate for your present and future needs. But remember, you should never examine any part of it without first switching off the power at the consumer unit. If you are in doubt about any aspect of the installation, don't hesitate to ask a qualified electrician for an opinion. If you get in touch with your electricity company, they will arrange for someone to test the whole system for you. It is recommended that you should have your house wiring tested at least every ten years.

Round-pin sockets
Replace old round-pin
sockets with 13amp
square-pin sockets.

Damaged sockets
Replace cracked or broken
faceplates.

Questions	Answers
Do you have a modern consumer unit, or a mixture of old fuse boxes?	Old fuse boxes can be unsafe and should be replaced with a modern unit. Seek professional advice about this.
Is the consumer unit in good condition?	Replace a broken casing or cracked covers. Trip MCBs deliberately every three months or so to make sure they are in good working order. Check that fuse carriers are intact and that they fit snugly in their fuseways.
Are all your MCBs or circuit fuses of the correct ratings?	Seek the advice of an electrician about replacing suspect MCBs. Replace any fuses of the wrong rating. If an unusually large fuse is protecting one of the circuits, don't change it without getting professional advice – it may have a special purpose. If you find any wire other than proper fuse wire in a fuse carrier, replace it at once. If you have rewirable fuses, ask an electrician to quote for having them converted to cartridge fuses or MCBs.
Are all the cables leading from the consumer unit in good condition?	The cables should be fixed securely, with no bare wires showing. If the cables appear to be insulated with rubber, have the whole installation checked as soon as possible. Rubber insulation has a limited life, so yours could already be dangerous.
Is the earth connection from the consumer unit intact and in good condition?	If the connection seems loose or corroded, have the electricity company check whether the earthing is sound. You can check an RCD by pushing the test button to make sure it is working mechanically.
What is the condition of the fixed wiring between floors and in the loft or roof space?	If just a few cables appear to be rubber-insulated, have the entire system checked by a professional – it can be confusing, as old cable may have been disconnected but left in place during a previous upgrade. If cable is run in conduit, it can be difficult to check on its condition – but if it looks doubtful where it enters the accessories, have the circuit checked professionally. Wiring should be fixed securely and sheathing should run into all accessories, with no bare wire in sight. Junction boxes on lighting or power circuits should be screwed firmly to the structure and should have their covers in place.
Is the wiring unobtrusive and orderly?	Tidy all surface-run wiring into properly clipped straight runs. Better still, bury the cable in the wall plaster or run it under floors and inside hollow walls.

SEE ALSO > Switching off 20, Old fuse boards 21, Consumer units 22, Fuse ratings 23, Running cable 27–9

Scorch marks
Scorch marks on a socket or round the base of plug pins indicate poor connections.

Warm plug
This is another indication of loose connections.

Overloaded socket
If you have to use adaptors to power your appliances, you should fit extra sockets.

Red and black insulation
This is perfectly safe, and merely suggests the wiring was installed before 2005.

Questions	Answers
Are there any old round-pin socket outlets?	Replace old radial circuits with modern wiring and 13amp square-pin sockets as soon as possible.
Are the outer casings of all accessories in good condition and fixed securely to the structure?	Replace any cracked or broken components and secure any loose fittings.
Do switches on all accessories work smoothly and effectively?	If the switches are not working properly, replace the accessories.
Are all the conductors inside accessories connected securely to their terminals?	Tighten all loose terminals and ensure no bare wires are visible. Fit green-and-yellow sleeves to earth wires if not fitted already.
Is the insulation around wires inside any accessories dry and crumbly?	If so, it is rubber insulation in advanced decomposition. Replace the covers carefully and have a professional check the system as soon as possible.
Are the wires in some accessories covered with red and black insulation?	This is perfectly safe. Only homes rewired after 2005 are likely to have cables with brown and blue insulation.
Do any sockets, switches or plugs feel warm? Is there a smell of burning? Or are there scorch marks visible on sockets or around the base of plug pins? Does a socket spark when you pull out a plug? Or a switch when you operate it?	All these symptoms mean loose connections in the accessory or plug, or a poor connection between plug and socket. Tighten loose connections and clean all fuse clips, fuse caps and plug pins with silicon-carbide paper, then wipe them with a soft cloth. If the fault persists, try fitting a new plug. If that fails to cure the problem, replace the socket or switch.
Is it difficult to insert a plug in a socket?	The socket is worn and should be replaced.
Are your sockets in the right places?	Sockets should be placed conveniently round a room so that you need never have long flexes trailing across the floor or under carpets. Add sockets to the ring circuit by running spurs.
Do you have enough sockets?	If you have to use plug adaptors, you need more sockets. Replace singles with doubles or add spurs.
Is there old twisted twin flex hanging from the ceiling roses?	Replace it with PVC-insulated-and-sheathed flex.
Are there earth wires inside your ceiling roses?	If not, get professional advice on whether to replace the lighting circuits.
Is you lighting efficient?	Consider extra sockets or different light fittings to make your lighting more effective. Make sure you have two-way switches on stairs.
Is there power in the garage or workshop?	Detached buildings should have their own power supply.

SEE ALSO > Colour coding 9, Flex 16, Plugs 19, Switching off 20, Old fuse boards 21, Consumer units 22, Fuse ratings 23, Running cable 27–9, Sockets 30, Ceiling roses 48, Running power to an outbuilding 66–7

20201480

Simple replacements

You can carry out many repairs and replacements without having to concern yourself with the wiring system installed in your home. Many light fittings and appliances are supplied with electricity by means of flexible cords that plug into the system – so provided that they have been disconnected, there can be no risk of getting an electric shock while working on them.

WARNING
Never attempt to carry out electrical repairs without first unplugging the appliance or switching off the power supply at the consumer unit.

Flexible cord (flex)

All portable appliances and some of the smaller fixed ones, as well as pendant and portable light fittings, are connected to your home's permanent wiring system by means of conductors in the form of flexible cord, normally called 'flex'.

Each of the conductors in any type of flex is made up of numerous fine wires twisted together, and each conductor is insulated from the others by a covering of plastic insulation. So that the conductors can be identified easily, the insulation is usually colour-coded (brown = live; blue = neutral; and green-and-yellow = earth). Further protection is provided on most flexible cords in the form of an outer sheathing of insulating material enclosing the inner conductors.

Heat-resistant flex is available for enclosed light fittings and appliances with surfaces that become hot.

Twisted twin flex
This is similar to parallel twin flex (above right), but the insulated conductors are twisted together for extra strength. It was once used to support hanging light fittings, but nowadays must be replaced with a two-core sheathed flex when wiring pendant lights.

Types of electrical flex

Parallel twin
Parallel twin flex has two conductors, insulated with PVC (polyvinyl chloride), running side by side. The insulation material is joined between the two conductors along the length of the flex. This kind of flex should only be used for wiring audio-equipment speakers. One of the conductors will be colour-coded for identification.

Flat twin sheathed
Flat twin sheathed flex has colour-coded live and neutral conductors inside a PVC sheathing. This flex is used for double-insulated light fittings and small appliances.

Two-core circular sheathed
This has colour-coded live and neutral conductors inside a PVC sheathing that is circular in its cross section. It is used for wiring certain pendant lights and some double-insulated appliances.

Three-core circular sheathed
This is like two-core circular sheathed flex, but it also contains an insulated and colour-coded earth wire. This flex is perhaps the most commonly used for all kinds of appliances. A special high-temperature flex is available for connecting immersion heaters, storage heaters and similar appliances.

Unkinkable braided
This flex is used for appliances such as kettles and irons, which are of a high wattage and whose flex must stand up to movement and wear. The three rubber-insulated conductors, plus the textile cords that run parallel with them, are all contained in a rubber sheathing that is bound outside with braided material. This type of flex can be wound round the handle of a cool electric iron.

Coiled flex
A coiled flex that stretches and retracts can be a convenient way of connecting a portable lamp or appliance.

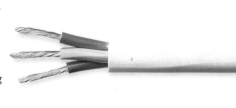

SEE ALSO > Colour coding 9, Extending flex 18

Connecting flexible cord

Although the spacing of terminals in plugs and appliances varies, the method of stripping and connecting the flex is the same.

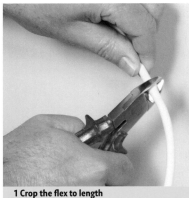

1 Crop the flex to length

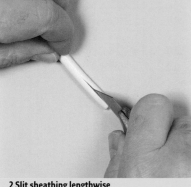

2 Slit sheathing lengthwise

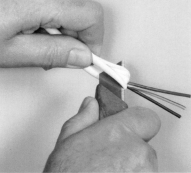

3 Fold sheathing over the blade and cut it off

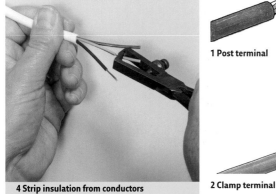

4 Strip insulation from conductors

Stripping the flex

Crop the flex to length (**1**). Slit the sheath lengthwise with a sharp knife (**2**), being careful not to cut into the insulation covering the individual conductors. Peel the sheathing away from the conductors, then fold it back over the knife blade and cut it off (**3**).

Separate the conductors, crop them to length and, using wire strippers, remove about 12mm (½in) of insulation from the end of each one (**4**).

Divide the conductors of parallel twin flex by pulling them apart before exposing their ends with wire strippers.

Connecting conductors

Twist together the individual filaments of each conductor to make them neat.

If the plug or appliance has post-type terminals, fold the bared wire (**1**) before pushing it into the hole. Make sure the insulation butts against the post and that all the wire filaments are enclosed within the terminal. Then tighten the clamping screw, and pull gently on the wire to make sure it is held quite firmly.

When you're connecting to clamp-type terminals, wrap the bared wire round the threaded post clockwise (**2**), then screw the clamping nut down tight onto the conductor. After tightening the nut, check that the conductor is held securely.

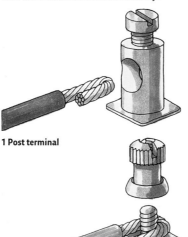

1 Post terminal

2 Clamp terminal

Choosing a flex

Not only is the right type of flex for the job important; the size of its conductors must suit the amount of current that will be used by the appliance.

Flex is rated according to the area of the cross section of its conductors, $0.5mm^2$ being the smallest for normal domestic wiring. The flex size required is determined by the flow of current that it can handle safely. Excessive current will make a conductor overheat – so the size of the flex must be matched to the power (wattage) of the appliance that it is feeding.

Manufacturers often fit $1.25mm^2$ flex to appliances of less than 3000W (3kW), since it is safer to use a larger conductor than necessary if a smaller flex might be easily damaged. It is advisable to adopt the same procedure when replacing flex.

Conductor	Current rating	Appliance
$0.5mm^2$	3amp	Light fittings up to 690W
$0.75mm^2$	6amp	Light fittings and appliances up to 1380W
$1.0mm^2$	10amp	Appliances up to 2300W
$1.25mm^2$	13amp	Appliances up to 2990W
$1.5mm^2$	15amp	Appliances up to 3450W
$2.5mm^2$	20amp	Appliances up to 4600W

Because they generate relatively high background temperatures, 3kW immersion heaters are wired with $2.5mm^2$ heat-resistant flex (see WIRING AN IMMERSION HEATER).

Wire strippers

Special tools are available for removing the plastic insulation covering flex and cable conductors. Traditional wire strippers have shaped jaws that cut through the covering without damaging the conductors.

Modern wire strippers have jaws calibrated in millimetres and inches to measure the amount of insulation to be removed. The single action of squeezing the handles cuts through the covering and then removes it.

SEE ALSO > Immersion heaters 40–1, Extending flex 18

Extending flexible cord

When you plan the positions of socket outlets, try to ensure there will be enough – all conveniently situated, so it's never necessary to extend the flexible cord of a table lamp or other appliance. But if you do find that a flex will not reach a socket, extend it so it is not stretched taut, which could cause an accident. Never be tempted to join two lengths of flex by twisting the bared ends of wires together, even if you bind them with insulating tape. People often do this as a temporary measure then neglect to make a proper connection later.

Flex connectors

● **Two-part flex connectors**
Connectors with two pins, as shown right, must only be used with two-core flex and double-insulated appliances.

If possible, fit a longer flex, wiring it into the appliance itself. But if you can't do this or don't want to dismantle the appliance, use a flex connector. There are two-terminal and three-terminal connectors, which you must match to the type of flex you are using. Never join two-core flex to three-core flex.

Strip off just enough sheathing for the conductors to reach the terminals, and make sure the sheathed part of each cord can be secured under the cord clamp at each end of the connector.

Crop the conductors to length, then strip and connect the conductors – connecting the live conductor to one of the outer terminals, the neutral to the other, and the earth wire (if present) to the central terminal. Make sure that matching conductors from both cords are connected to the same terminals, then tighten the cord clamps and screw the cover in place.

In-line switches

● **Larger appliances**
Never extend the flex of large appliances, such as dishwashers or washing machines. And don't plug them into an extension lead or trailing socket.

If you plan to fit a longer continuous length of flex you can install an in-line switch that will allow you to control the appliance or light fitting from some distance away – a great advantage for the elderly and people confined to bed. Some in-line switches are luminous.

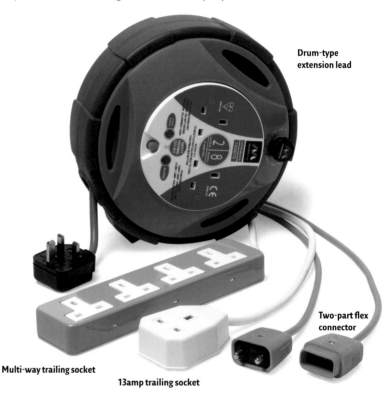

Drum-type extension lead

Two-part flex connector

Multi-way trailing socket

13amp trailing socket

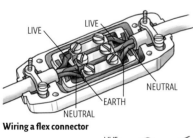

LIVE
LIVE
NEUTRAL
EARTH
NEUTRAL
Wiring a flex connector

LIVE
LIVE
NEUTRAL
Wiring an in-line switch

Extension leads

If you fit a long flex to a power tool, it will inevitably become tangled and one of the conductors will eventually break, perhaps causing a short circuit. The solution is to buy an extension lead or make one yourself.

The best type of extension lead to be had commercially is wound on a drum. There are 5amp ones – but it's safer to buy one with a 13amp rating, so you can run a wider range of equipment without danger of overloading. If you use such a lead while it is wound on the drum it may overheat, so develop the habit of unwinding it fully each time you plug in an appliance rated at 1kW or more. The drums of these leads have built-in 13amp sockets to take the plugs of appliances; the plug at the end of the lead is then connected to a wall socket.

You can make an extension lead from a length of 1.5mm² three-core flex with a standard 13amp plug on one end and a

trailing socket on the other. Use those with unbreakable rubber casings. A trailing socket is wired in a similar way to a 13amp plug (see opposite). Its terminals are marked to indicate which conductors to connect to them.

'Multi-way' trailing sockets will take several plugs and are ideal for hi-fi systems or computers with a number of individual components that need to be connected to the mains supply. Using a multi-way socket, the whole system is supplied with power from a single plug in the wall socket.

You can also extend a lead by using a two-part detachable flex connector. One half has pins that fit into the other half of the connector. When wiring a two-part flex connector, never attach the part with the pins to the extension lead. The exposed pins will become live – and dangerous – when the lead is plugged into the socket.

SEE ALSO ▸ Types of flex 16, Connecting flex 17

Replacing a pendant lampholder

Because pendant lampholders hang on a flexible cord from the ceiling, they are in a stream of hot air rising from the bulb. In time this tends to make plastic holders brittle and more easily cracked or broken. Check their condition from time to time, and replace any that look suspect before they become dangerous.

Plastic lampholders

Plastic lampholders are the most common type. They have a threaded skirt that screws onto the actual holder (the part that takes the bulb). Some have an extended skirt. If you are going to use a close-fitting or badly ventilated shade, fit a heat-resistant version. Plastic holders are designed to take two-core flex only. Never fit one on a three-core flex, as there is no place to attach the earth wire.

Where possible, replace an old metal lampholder with a plastic version, substituting its three-core flex with a two-core circular sheathed type.

Fitting a lampholder

Before commencing work, remove the circuit fuse or remove (or lock off) the circuit breaker from the consumer unit so that no-one can turn the power on.

Unscrew the old holder's cap and slide it up the flex to expose the terminals. Loosen their screws and pull the wires out. If some wires are broken or brittle, cut back slightly to expose sound wires before fitting the new holder.

Slide the cap of the new fitting up the flex and attach it temporarily with adhesive tape. Fit the live wire into one of the terminals, and the neutral wire into the other one. Then loop the conductors round the supporting lugs of the holder, to take the weight off the terminals, and screw the cap down.

FLEX

CAP

NEUTRAL

LIVE

Wiring a plastic pendant lampholder
This type of lampholder is for a bayonet-fitting bulb. When replacing a lampholder for an Edison-screw bulb, the live conductor from the flex must be connected to the central terminal of the holder.

SKIRT

• **Disposing of plugs**
Before you discard a damaged plug, bend one of the pins to prevent it being plugged into a socket by a child.

Three-pin plugs

Square-pin 13amp plugs are used to connect most portable light fittings and appliances to the mains supply. Their construction may vary slightly, but all 13amp plugs work on the same principle. They are available with plastic or rubber casings, and some have insulated pins to prevent the user getting a shock from a plug pulled partly from the socket. Use only plugs marked BS 1363.

Factory-fitted plugs

All new appliances are sold with a plug moulded onto the end of the flexible cord. This type of plug contains a small replaceable cartridge fuse within a retractable holder positioned between the pins. Factory-fitted plugs cannot be dismantled, so if you ever need to replace one that is damaged, cut through the flex and fit a rewirable plug.

Rewirable plugs

The plugs available in shops and DIY stores can be fitted onto any electrical flex. They too contain a replaceable cartridge fuse, which is accessible when the plug's cover is removed. All rewirable plugs have a cord clamp or grip that prevents the conductors being accidentally pulled out of their terminals.

Fuses for plugs

Use a 3amp (red) fuse for appliances of up to 720W, and a 13amp (brown) fuse for those of 720 to 3000W (3kW). There are also 2, 5 and 10amp fuses, but these are less often used in the home.

Wiring a 13amp plug

Loosen the large screw between the pins and remove the cover. Position the flex on the open plug to gauge how much sheathing to remove (the cord clamp must grip sheathed flex, not the conductors). Strip the sheathing and position the flex on the plug again, so that you can cut the conductors to the right length. These should take the most direct routes to their terminals and lie neatly within the channels of the plug.

Strip and prepare the ends of the wires, then secure each to its terminal. If you are using two-core flex, simply leave the earth terminal empty.

Tighten the cord clamp to grip the end of the sheathing and secure the flex (a sprung cord grip tightens if the flex is pulled hard). Fit a fuse of the correct rating , then replace the plug's cover and tighten up the screw.

Factory-fitted plug

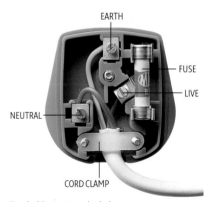

Rewirable plug

EARTH

FUSE

LIVE

NEUTRAL

CORD CLAMP

Rewirable post-terminal plug

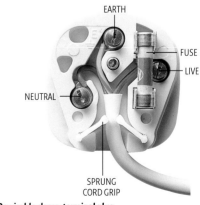

EARTH

FUSE

LIVE

NEUTRAL

SPRUNG CORD GRIP

Rewirable clamp-terminal plug

SEE ALSO > Connecting flex 17, Switching off 20, Light bulbs 50–1

Main switch equipment

Electricity flows because of a difference in 'pressure' between the live wire and the neutral one, and this difference in pressure is measured in volts. Domestic electricity in this country is supplied as alternating current, at 230 volts, by way of the electricity company's main service cable. This normally enters your house underground, although in some areas electricity is distributed by overhead cables.

The service head

• **Cross-bonding cable sizes**
Single-core cables are used to cross-bond gas and water pipes to earth. An electrician can calculate the minimum size for these cables, but for any single house or flat it is safe to use 10mm² cable. (See also PME opposite).

The main cable terminates at the service head, or 'cutout', which contains the service fuse. This fuse prevents the neighbourhood's supply being affected if there should be a serious fault in the circuitry of your house. Cables connect the cutout to the meter, which registers how much electricity you consume. Both the meter and cutout belong to the electricity company and must not be tampered with. The meter is sealed in order to disclose interference.

If you are using cheap night-time power for electric storage heaters and hot water, a time switch will be supplied by the electricity company.

Consumer unit

Electricity is fed to and from the consumer unit by 'meter leads', thick single-core insulated-and-sheathed cables made up of several wires twisted together. The consumer unit is a box containing the fuseways that protect the individual circuits in the house. It also incorporates the main isolating switch, which you operate when you need to cut off the supply of power to the whole house. Not all main isolating switches operate the same way. Before you need to use it, check to see whether the main switch on your consumer unit has to be in the up or down position for 'off'.

In a house where several new circuits have been installed over the years, the number of circuits may exceed the number of fuseways in the consumer unit. If so, an individual switchfuse unit – or more than one – may have been mounted alongside the main unit. Switchfuse units comprise a single fuseway and an isolating switch; they, too, are connected to the meter by means of meter leads.

If your home is heated by off-peak storage heaters, then you will have an Economy 7 meter and a separate consumer unit for the heater circuits.

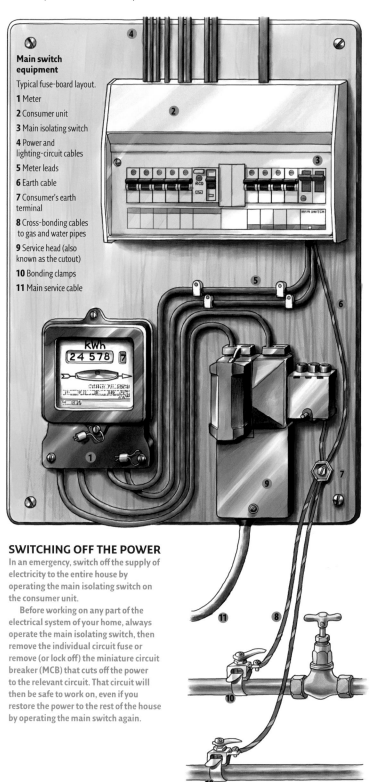

Main switch equipment
Typical fuse-board layout.
1 Meter
2 Consumer unit
3 Main isolating switch
4 Power and lighting-circuit cables
5 Meter leads
6 Earth cable
7 Consumer's earth terminal
8 Cross-bonding cables to gas and water pipes
9 Service head (also known as the cutout)
10 Bonding clamps
11 Main service cable

KWh
24 578

SWITCHING OFF THE POWER
In an emergency, switch off the supply of electricity to the entire house by operating the main isolating switch on the consumer unit.

Before working on any part of the electrical system of your home, always operate the main isolating switch, then remove the individual circuit fuse or remove (or lock off) the miniature circuit breaker (MCB) that cuts off the power to the relevant circuit. That circuit will then be safe to work on, even if you restore the power to the rest of the house by operating the main switch again.

SEE ALSO > Consumer units 22, Domestic circuits 25

Earthing and bonding

All of the individual earth conductors of the various circuits in the house are connected to a metal earthing block in the consumer unit. A single cable with a green-and-yellow covering runs from this earthing block to the consumer's earth terminal, which is mounted next to the cutout. In most urban houses a connection is provided from inside the cutout to an external earth-connection block, which is also wired to the consumer's earth terminal. This provides an effective path to earth, as it allows the current to pass along the sheath of the main service cable to the electricity company's substation, where it is solidly connected to earth. If the company does not provide an earth connection to its cable, the installation must be protected by an RCD.

In the past most domestic electrical systems were earthed to the cold-water supply, so earth-leakage current passed out along the metal water pipes into the ground in which they were buried. But nowadays more and more water systems use nonconductive, nonmetallic pipes and fittings. As a result, such a means of earthing is no longer reliable.

Despite this, you will find that your gas and water pipework is connected to the consumer's earth terminal. This ensures that the water and gas piping systems are cross-bonded, so earth-leakage current passing through either system will run without hindrance to the main earth without producing dangerously high voltages. The cross-bonding clamps must be as close as possible to the point where the pipes enter the house, but on the consumer's side (within 600mm) of the stopcock or gas meter.

Bonding clamp
This type of clamp (BS 951) is used to make connections to gas and water pipes. It must not be removed under any circumstances.

PME

The electricity company sometimes provides a different method of earthing the system, called 'protective multiple earth' (PME), by which earth-leakage current is fed back to the substation along the neutral return wire, and so to earth. Regulations regarding the earthing of this system are particularly stringent. With PME, cross-bonding cables to gas and water services are sometimes required to be larger. Check this with the electricity company.

RCDs

Although the local electricity company normally provides effective earthing for the electrical system of your home, safe earthing is the consumer's own responsibility. With this in mind, it is worth installing a residual current device (RCD) into the house circuitry.

When conditions are normal, the current flowing out through the neutral conductor is exactly the same as that flowing in through the live one. Should there be an imbalance between the two caused by an earth leakage, the residual current device will detect it immediately and isolate the circuitry.

An RCD can be either installed as a

A separate unit containing an RCD

separate unit or incorporated into the consumer unit, sometimes together with the main isolating switch.

A residual current device is sometimes referred to as a residual current circuit breaker (RCCB). It was formerly known as an ELCB, or earth-leakage circuit breaker.

Old fuse boards

Domestic wiring systems were once very different from the ones used today. Besides lighting, water-heating and cooker circuits, each socket outlet had its own circuit and fuse, while further circuits would be installed from time to time as the needs of the household changed. Consequently, an old house may have a mixture of 'fuse boxes' attached to the fuse board, along with the meter.

You may find that the wiring itself is haphazard and badly labelled, with the serious danger that you may not safely isolate a circuit you're going to work on. Furthermore, you will not be able to tell whether a particular fuse is correctly and safely rated unless you know what type of circuit it is protecting.

Arrange for an inspection

If your home still has such an old-style fuse board, have it inspected and tested by a qualified electrician before you attempt to work on any part of the system. He or she can advise you as to whether your installation needs to be replaced with a modern consumer unit. At the same time, check that the cables are PVC-insulated. If everything does prove to be in good working condition, he or she can label the various circuits clearly to help you in the future.

An old-fashioned fuse board
This type of installation is out of date. A professional electrician may advise you to replace at least some of the components.

SEE ALSO > Bathroom safety 10

Consumer units

The consumer unit is the heart of your electrical installation: every circuit in your home has to pass through it. Although there are several different types and styles, all consumer units are based on similar principles.

• Important notes
Make a note of the last time you had your electrical installation checked professionally, and attach it as close as possible to the consumer unit. Similarly, jot down the next proposed date of inspection.

If your home is wired with both the old-style colour-coded cables and the newer ones, attach a note near the consumer unit to alert anyone working on the fixed wiring of your house in the future.

Every consumer unit has a large main isolating switch, which can turn off the entire electrical system of the house. On some units, the switch is in the form of an RCD that can be operated manually but which will also 'trip' automatically should any serious fault occur, isolating the whole system. There is greater emphasis these days on protecting only the most vulnerable circuits with an RCD. With these 'split' consumer units, the main isolating switch still turns off every circuit simultaneously.

Some consumer units are designed in

such a way that it's impossible to remove the outer cover without first turning off the main isolating switch. Even if yours is not this type, always switch off the power before exposing any of the elements within the consumer unit.

Having turned off the main switch, remove the cover so that you can see how the unit is arranged. Remember that even when the unit is switched off the cable connecting the meter to the main switch is still live – so take care.

Take note of the cables that feed the

various circuits in the house. The blue-insulated neutral wires run to a common neutral block, where they are attached to their individual terminals. Similarly, the green-and-yellow earth wires run to a common earth block. The brown-covered live conductors are connected to terminals on individual fuseways or circuit breakers.

Some wires will be joined together in a single terminal. These are the two ends of a ring circuit, and that is how they should be wired.

EARTH BLOCK   **CIRCUIT CABLES**   **NEUTRAL BLOCK**   **METER LEADS**

UPSTAIRS LIGHTING CIRCUIT   **GARAGE CIRCUIT**   **RESIDUAL CURRENT DEVICE**   **BURGLAR ALARM**   **MAIN SWITCH**

IMMERSION-HEATER CIRCUIT   **UPSTAIRS POWER CIRCUIT**   **KITCHEN POWER CIRCUIT**   **COOKER CIRCUIT**   **DOWNSTAIRS LIGHTING CIRCUIT**   **UNCONNECTED MCB**

Split consumer unit with miniature circuit breakers
Only the circuits on the left are protected by the RCD.

DOWNSTAIRS POWER CIRCUIT   **EARTH LEAD**

SEE ALSO > Colour coding 9, Main switch equipment 20, Power failure 24, Domestic circuits 25, Cable 26

Fuses and circuit breakers

In some consumer units there is a fuseway for each circuit. Into each fuseway is plugged a fuse carrier, which is essentially a bridge between the main switch and that particular circuit. When the fuse carrier is removed from the consumer unit, the current cannot pass across the gap. In many consumer units you will find miniature circuit breakers (MCBs) instead of fuse carriers.

Identifying fuses

Pull any fuse carrier out of the consumer unit and turn it round to see what kind of fuse it contains.

At each end of the carrier you will see a single-bladed or double-bladed contact. An old rewirable carrier will have a thin wire running from one contact to the other, held by a screw terminal at each end. Fuse wire is made in various thicknesses, calculated to melt at given currents when a circuit is substantially overloaded, thus breaking the 'bridge' and isolating the circuit.

Alternatively, the carrier may contain a cartridge fuse, varying in size according to its rating. The cartridge is a ceramic tube containing a fuse wire packed in fine sand. The wire is connected to metal caps at the ends of the cartridge that snap into spring clips on the contacts of the fuse carrier.

Cartridge fuses provide better protection, since they blow faster than ordinary fuse wire; modern consumer units no longer contain rewirable fuses.

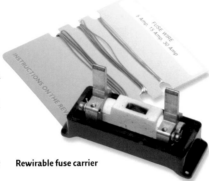

Rewirable fuse carrier

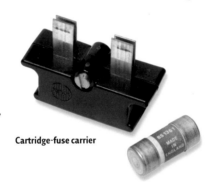

Cartridge-fuse carrier

Fuse ratings

Whatever the type of fuses used in the consumer unit, they are rated in the same way. Cartridge fuses are colour-coded and marked with the appropriate amp rating for a certain type of circuit. Fuse wire is bought wrapped round a clearly labelled card.

Never insert fuse wire that is heavier than the gauge intended for the circuit. To do so could result in a dangerous fault going unnoticed because the fuse wire fails to melt. And it is even more dangerous to substitute any other type of wire or metal strip; these provide no protection at all.

When you need to change a fuse, do not automatically replace it with one of the same rating. Check first that it is the correct type of fuse for the circuit. The fuse carrier should be marked and/or colour-coded. You can also look at the list of circuits printed on the inside of the consumer-unit cover to identify the carriers and their required ratings.

Keep spare fuse wire or cartridge fuses in or close to the consumer unit.

Miniature circuit breakers

With MCBs a faulty circuit is obvious as soon as you inspect the consumer unit, as they switch to the 'off' position automatically. There are many types of miniature circuit breaker on the market, but only buy ones made to the required standards of construction and safety.

Make sure any MCB that you use is marked BS EN 60898, which is the relevant British Standard. There are also different classes of MCB (you need to look for Type B). And lastly, MCBs are classified according to the largest potential fault current they are able to clear; ask for M6 or M9, as these will clear any potential current likely to be met in a domestic situation.

MCB ratings

To conform to European standards, MCB ratings tend to vary slightly from circuit-fuse ratings (see CIRCUITS: MAXIMUM LENGTHS). However, if you have MCBs that match the slightly smaller ratings shown for circuit fuses, that is perfectly acceptable.

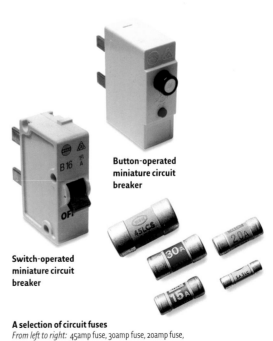

Button-operated miniature circuit breaker

Switch-operated miniature circuit breaker

A selection of circuit fuses
From left to right: 45amp fuse, 30amp fuse, 20amp fuse, 15amp fuse, 5amp fuse.

FUSE RATINGS		
Circuit	**Fuse**	**Colour coding**
Door bell	5amp	White
Lighting	5amp	White
Immersion heater	15amp	Blue
Storage heater	15amp	Blue
Radial circuits – 20sq m maximum floor area	20amp	Yellow
50sq m maximum floor area	30amp	Red
Ring circuits – 100sq m maximum floor area	30amp	Red
Shower unit	45amp	Green
Cooker	30amp	Red

SEE ALSO > Power failure 24, Domestic circuits 25, Circuit lengths 68

In the event of a power failure

If there's a fault on a circuit or it is overloaded by having too many appliances plugged into it, the MCB protecting the circuit will 'trip' (switch to the 'off' position); or if the circuit is protected by a fuse, the fuse will 'blow' (melt). When everything on a circuit stops working, go to your consumer unit and look for a tripped MCB or a blown fuse. However, if all or any of the circuits are protected by an RCD, check first to see whether the RCD has switched off.

Identifying the faulty circuit

If your RCD has tripped, turn off all the MCBs it is protecting and then reset the RCD. Now turn on each MCB in turn until the RCD trips again. Having identified the faulty circuit, turn off the consumer unit's main switch and tape it in the 'off' position while you are working. Inspect the sockets or light fittings and switches on the suspect circuit to see if a conductor has worked loose and is touching one of the other wires or terminals or the outer casing, causing a short circuit. If that doesn't solve the problem, keep the faulty circuit isolated (MCB locked off) and call in an electrician.

Resetting an MCB

• **Regular testing**
It is a good idea to check that all your MCBs and RCDs are in good working order by tripping them deliberately every three months or so. If an MCB has tripped frequently, have it replaced.

Assuming your RCD is still switched on when you inspect your consumer unit, look next for a miniature circuit breaker that has switched automatically to the 'off' position; or if your MCBs are the press-button type, see whether a button has popped out. If so, turn off the consumer unit's main switch, and reset the MCB by moving the toggle switch to the 'on' position (**1**) or pressing the button back in. Then turn the main switch on again (**2**).

If the same MCB trips immediately, unplug or switch off everything on the circuit to make sure the cause is not simply overloading or a faulty appliance, then reset the MCB as before. If the MCB trips again, look for loose connections as described above and then, if necessary, get an electrician to trace and rectify the fault.

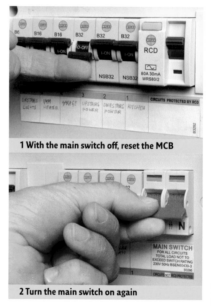
1 With the main switch off, reset the MCB

2 Turn the main switch on again

Replacing a cartridge fuse

Turn off the main switch on the consumer unit, take off the cover, and look for the failed fuse. To identify the relevant fuse, look at the list of circuits inside the cover. If there is no list, inspect the most likely circuits. If, for example, the lights blew when you switched them on, you need check only the lighting circuits, which are usually colour-coded white.

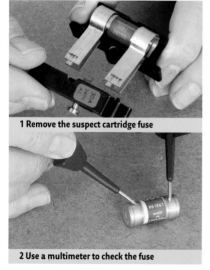
1 Remove the suspect cartridge fuse

2 Use a multimeter to check the fuse

Checking a cartridge fuse

With the power turned off, pull out the suspect fuse carrier and then, depending on the style of the fuse carrier, either dismantle the carrier to gain access to the cartridge fuse (**1**) or prise the fuse out of its spring clips.

Check the fuse with a multimeter set to its lowest resistance range. Place one of the meter's probes on each of the fuse's metal caps (**2**). If the meter reading is high (thousands of Ohms or more), the fuse has blown. Insert a new fuse of the appropriate rating and replace the carrier, then turn on the main switch.

Checking a rewirable fuse

Broken fuse wire is usually obvious, but if you can't be sure, pull gently on each end of the wire with the tip of a small screwdriver to see if the wire is intact (**1**).

Replacing fuse wire

To replace blown fuse wire, loosen the two terminals holding the old wire and extract the broken pieces. Wrap one end of a new length of the correct fuse wire clockwise round one of the terminals (**2**) and tighten the screw. Attach the other end to the second terminal, making sure you don't stretch the wire taut. Tighten the screw, cut off excess wire from the ends, then replace the fuse carrier. Turn on the main switch.

1 Pull the wire gently with a small screwdriver

2 Wind the wire clockwise round the terminal

Checking out a fault

If a fuse (of either type) blows again as soon as the power is restored, then there is either a fault or an overload on that circuit. Unplug or switch off everything on the circuit to make sure it isn't overloaded, then replace the fuse again. If the same fuse blows immediately, turn off the main switch and check for loose connections on the circuit as described above left. If you can't find the fault, call in an electrician.

SEE ALSO > Consumer units 22, Fuses and circuit breakers 23

CIRCUITS DOMESTIC 25

Domestic circuits

Running from the consumer unit are the cables that supply the various fixed wiring circuits in your home. Not only are the sizes of the cables different, the circuits themselves also differ, depending on what they are used for and also, in some cases, how old they happen to be.

Ring circuits

The most common form of 'power' circuit for feeding socket outlets is the ring circuit, or 'ring main'. With this method of wiring, a cable starts from terminals in the consumer unit and goes round the house, connecting socket to socket and arriving back at the same terminals. This means that power can reach any of the socket outlets or fused connection units from both directions, which reduces the load on the cable.

Ring mains are always run in 2.5mm² cable and are protected by 30amp fuses or 32amp MCBs. Theoretically there is no limit to the number of socket outlets or fused connection units that can be fitted to a ring circuit provided that it does not serve a floor area of more than 100sq m (120sq yd) – a limit based on the number of heaters that would be adequate to warm that space. However, in practice two-storey houses usually have one ring main for the upper floor and another one for downstairs.

Spurs

The number of sockets on a ring main can be increased by adding extensions or 'spurs'. A spur can be either a single 2.5mm² cable connected to the terminals of an existing socket or fused connection unit (FCU), or it can run from a junction box inserted in the ring.

Each (unfused) spur can feed only one fused connection unit for a fixed appliance or one single or double socket outlet. You can have as many unfused spurs on a ring circuit as there were sockets or FCUs on it originally (note that for this calculation a double socket is counted as two).

The 30amp fuse (or 32amp MCB) that protects the ring main remains unchanged, no matter how many spurs are connected to the circuit.

Radial circuits

A radial power circuit feeds a number of sockets or fused connection units – but, unlike a ring circuit, its cable terminates at the last outlet. The size of cable and the fuse rating depend on the size of the floor area to be supplied by the circuit. In an area of up to 20sq m (24sq yd), the cable needs to be 2.5mm², protected by a 20amp MCB or a 20amp fuse of any type. For a larger area, up to 50sq m (60sq yd), you should use 4mm² cable with a 30amp cartridge fuse or 32amp MCB (a rewirable fuse is not permitted).

Any number of socket outlets can be supplied by one of these circuits, and spurs can be added if required. These circuits are known as multi-outlet radial circuits. A powerful appliance such as a cooker or shower unit must have its own radial circuit.

Lighting circuits

Domestic lighting circuits are of the radial kind, but there are two systems currently in use.

The loop-in system simply has a single cable that runs from ceiling rose to ceiling rose, terminating at the last one on the circuit. Single cables also run from the ceiling roses to the various light switches.

The junction-box system (which is the older of the two systems) incorporates a junction box for each light. The boxes are situated conveniently on the single supply cable. A cable runs from each junction box to the ceiling rose, and another from the box to the light switch. In practice, most lighting circuits are a combination of the two methods.

A single circuit of 1.5mm² cable is able to serve the equivalent of eleven 100W light fittings. Check the load by adding together the wattage of all the light bulbs on the circuit. If the total comes to more than 1200W, the circuit should be split. In any case, it makes sense to have two or more separate lighting circuits running from the consumer unit.

Lighting circuits must be protected by 5amp fuses or 6amp MCBs.

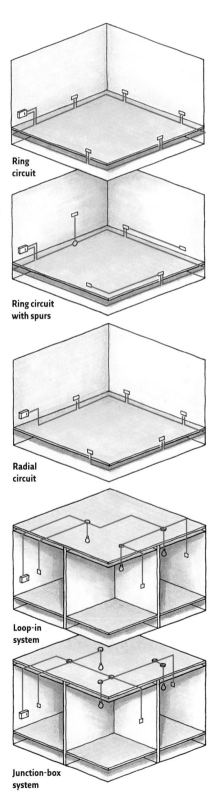

Ring circuit

Ring circuit with spurs

Radial circuit

Loop-in system

Junction-box system

SEE ALSO > Fuse ratings 23, Cables 26, Sockets 30, Fused connection units 34, Cooker circuits 38, Shower circuit 40, Circuit lengths 68

Electrical cable

Cable supplies power to every socket, switch and fixed appliance in your home. The conductors or wires in modern cable are invariably made from copper, and are insulated and sheathed in PVC. The insulation is colour-coded to identify live, neutral and earth conductors.

Types of domestic cable

A number of different types of electrical cable are found in domestic wiring.

Light-switch cabling

Two-core-and-earth cable

Cable for the fixed wiring in your home usually has three conductors: the insulated live and neutral ones and the earth conductor lying between them, which is uninsulated except for the sheathing that encloses all three conductors. Cable up to 2.5mm² has solid single-core conductors; but larger sizes (up to 10mm²) wouldn't be flexible enough if they had solid conductors, so each one is made up of seven strands. The live conductor is insulated with brown PVC, and the neutral one with blue. If the earth wire is exposed, as in a socket outlet, it should be covered with a green-and-yellow sleeve. The PVC sheathing on the outside of the cable is usually white or grey.

Prewar cable
Houses wired before World War II may still have old cable that is sheathed and insulated in rubber. Rubber sheathing is usually a matt black. It is more flexible than modern PVC insulation – unless it has deteriorated, in which case it will be crumbly. Old cable may be dangerous and needs to be replaced.

Three-core-and-earth cable

This cable is used for a two-way lighting system, which can be turned on and off at different switches – at the top and bottom of a staircase, for example. It contains three insulated conductors – with brown, black and grey coverings – and a bare earth wire.

Single-core cable

Insulated single-core cable is used in buildings where the electrical wiring is run in metal or plastic conduit – a type of installation rarely found in domestic buildings. The cable is colour-coded in the normal way: brown for live, blue for neutral, and green-and-yellow for earth.

Single-core 16mm² cable insulated in a green-and-yellow PVC covering is used for connecting the consumer unit to the earth. Single-core cable of the same size is used for connecting the consumer unit to the meter. The meter leads are insulated in brown for the live conductor and blue for the neutral one.

Light-switch cabling

Wall-mounted light switches are usually wired with ordinary 1.5mm² two-core-and-earth cable. The live wire is colour-coded brown, and the switch-return wire blue. Because the blue wire carries live current back to the light fitting, it is normal to either attach a brown flag or slip brown sheathing over the wire to identify it. However, you can now buy special cable with two brown wires for wiring light switches.

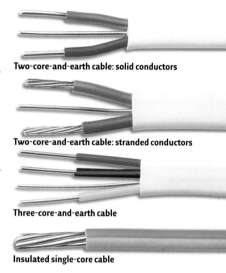

Two-core-and-earth cable: solid conductors

Two-core-and-earth cable: stranded conductors

Three-core-and-earth cable

Insulated single-core cable

Insulated-and-sheathed single-core cable

Cable sizes

The chart below gives the basic sizes of cables used for wiring domestic circuits. For details of the maximum permitted lengths for circuits, see CIRCUITS: MAXIMUM LENGTHS. If the company fuse is larger than 60amps, 25mm² meter leads are required – but it is best to consult your electricity company for advice.

Stripping cable

When cable is wired to an accessory, some of the sheathing and insulation must be removed. Slit the sheathing lengthwise with a sharp knife, peel it off the conductors, then fold it over the blade and cut it off. Take about 12mm (½ in) of insulation off the ends of the conductors, using wire strippers.

Cover the uninsulated earth wire with a green-and-yellow plastic sleeve, leaving 12mm (½ in) of the wire exposed.

If two stranded conductors are to be inserted in the same terminal, twist the exposed ends together with pliers. Don't twist solid conductors; simply insert them together into the terminal. Tighten the fixing screws, and pull on each conductor to make sure it is held securely.

CIRCUIT-CABLE SIZES		
Circuit	Size	Type
Fixed lighting	1.5mm²	Two-core-and-earth
Bell or chime transformer	1.5mm²	Two-core-and-earth
Immersion heater	2.5mm²	Two-core-and-earth
Storage heater	2.5mm² & 4.0mm²	Two-core-and-earth
Ring circuit	2.5mm²	Two-core-and-earth
Spurs	2.5mm²	Two-core-and-earth
Radial – 20amp	2.5mm²	Two-core-and-earth
Radial – 30amp	4.0mm²	Two-core-and-earth
Shower unit	10.0mm²	Two-core-and-earth
Cooker	4.0mm² & 6.0mm²	Two-core-and-earth
Consumer earth cable	16.0mm²	Single core
Meter leads	16.0mm²	Single core

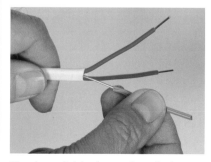

Slip colour-coded sleeving over the earth wire

SEE ALSO > Colour coding 9, Wire strippers 17, Earth lead 20, Meter leads 20, Two-way lighting 56, Circuit lengths 68

Running cable

Long runs of cable are necessary to carry electricity from the consumer unit to all the sockets, light fittings and fixed appliances in the home. Along its route the cable must be fixed securely to the structure of the house, except in confined spaces to which there is normally no access, such as inside hollow walls.

Surface fixing

Though it may be unsightly, PVC-sheathed cable can be fixed to the surface of a wall or ceiling without any further protection. Fix it with plastic cable clips or metal buckle clips every 400mm (1ft 4in) on vertical runs, and every 250mm (10in) on horizontal runs. Try to keep the runs straight, and avoid kinks in the cable by keeping it on the drum as long as possible. If you do have to remove kinks, pull the cable round a thick dowel held in a vice.

If a cable seems vulnerable, or you simply want to hide it, run it inside plastic mini-trunking. Screw or stick the trunking to the wall (see far right), then insert the cable and clip on the flexible cover strip.

Plastic cable clip

Metal buckle clip

Concealed fixing

While surface-fixed cable is acceptable in a cellar or in a garage or workshop, you wouldn't want to see it running across your living room walls or ceiling. From a decorative point of view, it's better to bury it in the plaster or hide it in a wall void. PVC-sheathed cable can be buried without further protection.

Where possible, run cable vertically to accessories such as switches or socket outlets, to avoid dangerous clashes with wall fixtures installed later. If that is not possible, you are permitted to run the cable horizontally directly from the switch or socket. However, if a cable isn't connected to a switch or socket on a wall in which it is concealed, then the cable must be within 150mm (6in) of the vertical or horizontal edges of the wall. Never, in any circumstances, run a buried cable diagonally across a wall.

Some people cover all buried cable with a plastic channel or run it inside conduit, but this is not required by the IEE Wiring Regulations. However, any cable that is buried in plastic conduit can, if necessary, be withdrawn later without having to damage the paintwork or wallcovering.

Mark out your cable runs on the plaster, making allowance for a 'chase', or channel, about 25mm (1in) wide for single cable. Cut both sides with a bolster and club hammer (**1**), and then use a cold chisel to hack out the plaster between the cuts. Normally, plaster is thick enough to conceal cable, but you may have to chop out some brickwork to get the depth. Clip the cable in the channel and, once you have checked that the installation is working properly, plaster over it (**2**). To avoid electric shock, ensure that the power is turned off before you use wet plaster round a switch or socket outlet.

Inside a hollow wall

To install a short cable run in a lath-and-plaster wall, hack the plaster away, fix the cable to the studs, and then plaster over again in the normal way.

Although you can run cable through the space between the two claddings of a partition wall, there is no way of doing this without at least some damage to the wall. Cut a hole in the plaster near the ceiling and directly above the spot where you are planning to position the switch, for example, and then drill a 12mm (½in) hole through the top head plate (**1**). Tap the wall directly below the hole to locate the nogging. Cut another hole in the plaster to reveal the top of the nogging, then drill a similar hole through it.

Pass a weight on a plumb line through both holes, down to where the switch will be. Tie the line to the cable, tape it and pull it through (**2**).

Plastic mini-trunking
Peel off the backing strip and stick the trunking to the wall plaster or paintwork.

1 Drill a hole through the head plate

2 Pull the cable through to the switch position

1 Cut a chase in the plaster for the cable

2 Repair the plaster up to the switch or socket

Running cable under floors

Power and lighting circuits are often concealed beneath floors. It isn't necessary to lift every floorboard to run a cable from one side of a room to the other: by lifting a board every 2m (6ft) or so, you should be able to pass the cable from one gap to the next with the help of a length of stiff wire bent into a hook at one end.

Lifting floorboards

Drive a wide bolster chisel between two boards about 50mm (2in) from the cut end of one of them (**1**). Lever that board up with the bolster, then do the same on the other edge, working along the board until you have raised it far enough to wedge a cold chisel under it (**2**). Proceed along the board, raising it with the chisel, till the board is loose.

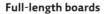

Lifting tongued boards
Use a special floorboard saw to cut through the tongue on both sides of the board.

Full-length boards
If you have to lift a board that runs the whole length of the floor from one skirting to the other, start somewhere near the middle of the board, close to one of the floor joists – the nail heads indicate the positions of joists. Lever the board up and make a sawcut across it, centred on the joist, then lift the board in the normal way.

Lifting tongue-and-groove boards
You cannot lift a tongue-and-groove floorboard until you have cut through the tongues along both sides of the board with a floorboard saw, which has a blade with a rounded tip.

1 Prise up the floorboard with a bolster

2 Wedge the raised end with a cold chisel

Cutting a board next to a skirting

A joist that is fitted close to a wall may make it impossible to lift a floorboard in the normal way without damaging the bottom edge of the skirting.

In such a case, drill a starting hole through the floorboard alongside the joist, then insert the blade of a padsaw into the hole and cut across the board, flush with the side of the joist (**1**).

To support the cut end afterwards, nail a length of 50 x 50mm (2 x 2in) softwood to the joist. Hold the batten tightly against the undersides of the adjacent floorboards while you are fixing it, to ensure that the cut board will lie flush with the others (**2**).

1 Cut through a trapped board with a padsaw

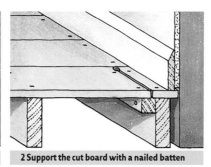
2 Support the cut board with a nailed batten

Solid floors

In a new concrete floor, you can lay conduit and then run cable through it before the concrete is poured.

In an existing solid floor, you can cut a channel for conduit, although it's hard work without an electric hammer and chisel bit; and if the floor is tiled, you will not want to spoil it for one or two socket outlets. An alternative is to drop spur cables, buried in the wall plaster, from the ring circuit in the upper floor.

Another way is to run cable through the wall from an adjacent area and channel it horizontally in the plaster just above the skirting. Yet another is to install plastic mini-trunking along the top of the skirting.

In the roof space

All wiring can be surface-run in the roof space; but as people may enter the space from time to time, you must make sure the cable is clipped securely to the joists or rafters. Run it through holes in the normal way, especially where joists are to be boarded over or in areas of access – around water tanks and near the entrance hatch, for example. If short lengths have to run on top of a joist, add mechanical protection.

Wiring overlaid by roof-insulation material has a slightly higher chance of heating up. Lighting circuits do not present a problem; but circuits on which there are heaters, cookers or shower units, for example, are more critical. Wherever possible, run cable over thermal insulation. If you cannot avoid running it under the material, use a heavier cable – but consult a qualified electrician to be on the safe side.

When expanded-polystyrene insulation is in contact with cable for a long time, it affects the plasticizer in the PVC sheathing on the cable. The plasticizer reacts with the polystyrene, forming a sticky substance on the cable. This becomes a dry crust, which can crack if the cable is moved. Although it gives the impression that the sheathing is cracking, scientific testing has shown that the cracking is in fact merely in the surface crust. On balance, however, it is best to keep cable away from polystyrene.

SEE ALSO > Mini-trunking 27, Spur cables 25, 33

Running cable through the house

Use the most convenient method to run cable to sockets and switches.

1 Clip cable to battens nailed to roof timbers in the loft.

2 Junction boxes must be fixed securely.

3 In the joists near the hatch, run cable through holes.

4 Run cable over loft insulation.

5 To avoid damaging a finished floor, you can run a short spur through the wall from the next room.

6 When cable needs to run across the line of joists, drill holes 50mm (2in) below the joists' top edges.

7 When cable needs to run parallel to the joists, it can lie on the ceiling below.

8 Let cable drape onto the base below a suspended floor.

9 If it's impractical to run cable through a concrete floor, you can drop a spur from the floor above, but label the consumer unit accordingly.

● **Labelling circuits**
If you have added sockets to a ring or radial circuit, make sure that the label in the consumer unit identifies the circuit to which the new sockets are connected.

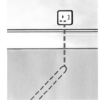

Burying cable in concrete
When you are laying a new concrete floor, take the opportunity to bury conduit for cable.

Running the cable

On the ground floor the cable can rest on the earth or on the concrete platform below the joists, provided that there won't normally be access to the space. Allow enough slack, so the cable isn't suspended above the platform, which might put a strain on fixings to junction boxes or socket outlets. For the same reason, beside junction boxes or other accessories, secure cable with clips to the side of the joist. Never attach circuit cable to gas or water pipes; and don't run it next to heating pipes, as the heat could melt the PVC sheathing and insulation.

When laying cable between a floor and the ceiling below, it can rest on the ceiling without any other fixing, so long as the cable runs parallel with the joists. If it runs at right angles to the joists, drill a series of 12mm (½in) holes, one through each joist along the intended cable run. The holes must be at least 50mm (2in) below the tops of the joists, so floorboard nails won't at some time be hammered through the cable. Similarly holes must be at least 50mm (2in) from the bottom edge of ceiling joists, in order to be certain that nails driven from below cannot pierce the cable. The space between joists is limited, but you can cut down a spade bit for use in a power drill.

Having marked out the position of a socket or fused connection unit, cut a channel from it down to the skirting board and, with a long masonry bit fitted in a power drill, remove the plaster from behind the skirting board. Use the drill at a shallow angle to loosen the debris, then finish the job with a slim cold chisel. Raking the debris out from below, with the same chisel, also helps to dislodge it.

Pass a length of stiff wire with one end formed into a hook down behind the skirting. Hook the cable and pull it through, at the same time feeding it from below with your other hand.

Drilling the joists
Shorten a spade bit so that your drill fits between the joists. Take care not to weaken joists.

Drilling behind skirting
Use an extra-long masonry bit to remove plaster behind a skirting board.

Preventing the spread of fire

Every time you cut an opening in the structure of the house for a cable, you are creating a potential route for fire and smoke to spread. After you have installed the cable, fill any holes between floors or rooms, using plaster or some other non-flammable material (not asbestos). Even where you pass a cable into a mounting box, you must fit a 'blind' grommet and cut a hole through it that is only just large enough for the cable.

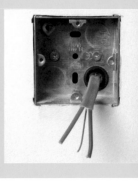

SEE ALSO > Cable clips 27, Concealing cable 27, Fitting a grommet 31, Running a spur 33

Socket outlets

Whatever type of circuits exist in your home, only use 13amp square-pin sockets. All round-pin sockets are now out of date – and even if they are not actually dangerous at the moment, you should have them checked and consider changing your wiring to accommodate 13amp sockets. Before you start work on any socket, switch the power off at the consumer unit and remove the fuse or remove (or lock off) the MCB for the relevant circuit – then test the socket with a mains-voltage tester to make sure the power has been switched off.

Switched single

Unswitched single

Single switched with indicator

Switched double

Types of 13amp socket

Although all sockets are functionally similar, there are several variations to choose from. For most situations, you are likely to use either a single or double socket. Both are available switched or unswitched, and with or without neon indicators so you can see at a glance whether the socket is switched on. All of these are wired in the same way.

Another basic difference is in how the sockets are mounted. They can either be surface-mounted (screwed to the wall in a plastic box) or flush-mounted in a metal box buried in the wall, with only the faceplate visible.

Positioning socket outlets

Choose the most convenient positions for hi-fi and computer equipment, table lamps, television, and so on, and position your sockets accordingly. To avoid using adaptors or long leads, distribute the sockets evenly round living rooms and bedrooms, and wherever possible fit doubles rather than singles. Don't forget sockets for running a vacuum cleaner in hallways and on landings.

Most sockets are mounted just above the skirting, between 225 and 300mm (9in to 1ft) from the floor. There is a recommendation that sockets should be between 450mm and 1.2m (1ft 6in to 4ft) above the floor, to make them accessible to a person using a wheelchair. If you want to install additional sockets at this higher level, simply run short vertical spurs from existing sockets.

In the kitchen, fit at least four double sockets 150mm (6in) above the work-tops. You will also need sockets for floor-standing appliances, such as refrigerators and dishwashers. You must inform your BCO before installing new sockets in a kitchen.

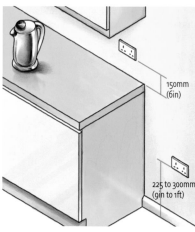

150mm (6in)

225 to 300mm (9in to 1ft)

Optimum heights for socket outlets

Surface-mounted socket outlets

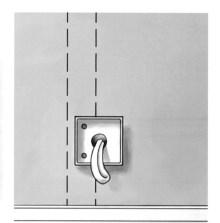

Triple sockets
Though relatively expensive, triple sockets are useful where several electrical appliances are grouped together.

Using a small screwdriver, break out the thin plastic webs that cover the fixing holes in the back of a plastic mounting box. Two fixings should be sufficient. The fixing holes are slotted to enable easy adjustment.

Hold the mounting box firmly against a masonry wall. Use a small spirit level to check that the box is upright, then mark the position of the fixing holes on the wall with a bradawl through the holes in the back of the box. Drill and plug the holes with No 8 wallplugs.

With a larger screwdriver and pliers, break out the plastic web covering the most convenient cable-entry hole in the box. For surface-run cable this will be in the side; for buried cable it will be the one in the base.

Feed the cable into the mounting box to form a loop about 75mm (3in) long, then fix the box to the wall with 32mm (1¼in) countersunk woodscrews. Finally, wire and fit the socket.

Leave a 75mm (3in) loop of cable at the box

Fixing to a hollow wall
On a dry-partition or lath-and-plaster wall, a surface-mounted box is fixed with any of the standard fixings used for hollow walls. Alternatively, use ordinary woodscrews if you are able to position the box over a stud, making sure you can feed the cable into the mounting box past the stud.

Feed the cable past the stud into the box

SEE ALSO > Switching off 20, Running cable 27–9, Wiring a socket 32, Circuit lengths 68

Flush-mounted sockets

Sockets that are fitted flush with the wall are not only better in appearance but are also less likely to get broken by being struck with vacuum cleaners and children's toys.

Fixing to masonry

Hold the metal box against the wall and draw round it with a pencil (**1**), then mark a 'chase' (channel) running up from the skirting to the box's outline.

Using a bolster or cold chisel, cut away the plaster down to the masonry (**2**), within the marked area. With a masonry bit, bore several rows of holes down to the required depth across the recess for the box (**3**); then, using a cold chisel, cut away the masonry to the depth of the holes, so that the box will lie flush with the plaster.

Try the box in the recess. If it fits in snugly, mark the wall through the fixing holes in its back, then drill the wall for screw plugs. If you have made the recess too deep or the box rocks from side to side, apply some filler in the recess and press the box into it, flush with the wall and properly positioned. After about 10 minutes, ease the box out carefully and leave the filler to harden, so that you can mark, drill and plug the fixing holes through it.

Next, knock out one or more of the blanked-off holes in the box to accommodate the cable. Fit a blind grommet into each hole to protect the cable's sheathing from the metal edges (**4**). Feed the cable into the box, and screw the box to the wall.

Plaster up to the box and over the cable chased into the wall; then, when the plaster has hardened, wire and fit the socket itself.

1 Draw round the mounting box

2 Chop away the plaster with a cold chisel

3 Drill out the blockwork with a masonry bit

4 Fit a soft grommet in the cable-entry hole

Fixing to plasterboard

In order to fit a flush socket to a wall made of plasterboard laid over wooden studs, trace the outline of the metal box on the wall and drill a hole in each corner. Then use a padsaw to cut out the recess for the box.

Punch out the blanked-off entry holes in the box and then line them with rubber grommets. Feed the cable into the box.

Clip dry-wall fixing flanges to the sides of the box – these will hold it in place by gripping the wall from inside (see also far right). Ease one side of the box, with flange, into the recess; and then, holding the screw-

Dry-wall fixing flanges clipped to a box

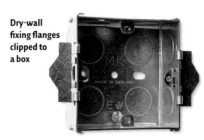

fixing lugs, manoeuvre the box until both flanges are behind the plasterboard and the box sits snugly in the hole. Wire and fit the socket and, as you tighten the fixing screws, the plasterboard will be gripped between the flanges and the faceplate.

Lath-and-plaster

Older homes have partition walls covered with thin strips of wood, known as laths, that form a key for the wall plaster. If you want to fit a flush socket outlet in a lath-and-plaster wall, try to locate it over a stud or nogging.

Mark the position of the metal box, cut out the plaster, and saw away the laths with a padsaw. Try the box for fit, and if necessary chop a notch in the woodwork until the box lies flush with the wall surface. Feed in the cable; and screw the box to the stud before wiring and fitting the socket.

If you can't position the socket on a stud, cut away enough of the plaster and laths to make a slot in the wall running from one stud to the next. Between the studs, screw or skew-nail a stout softwood nogging to which you can fix the box. If necessary, set the batten back from the front edges of the studs, to make the mounting box lie flush with the wall surface. Feed the cable into the box and make good the surrounding plaster before you wire and fit the socket.

Cavity-wall box
Instead of fitting dry-wall fixing flanges to a standard mounting box, you can use a special cavity-wall box with integral hinged flanges that you push through the sides of the box after it is fitted.

Notch a wall stud for the mounting box

Alternatively, nail a nogging between the studs

SEE ALSO > Switching off 20, Running cable 27–9, Wiring a socket 32

Replacing socket outlets

If you need to replace a broken or faulty socket, there are several options worth considering before you embark on the job. There is no need to notify your BCO before changing a damaged socket.

Simple replacement

Replacing a damaged socket with a similar one is a fairly straightforward job. A socket outlet of any style will fit into a metal mounting box, but check carefully when you substitute a socket that screws onto a surface-mounted plastic box. Although it will fit and function perfectly well, square corners and edges on either will not suit rounded ones on the other – in which case, you may also have to buy a new, matching box.

An unswitched socket outlet can be replaced with a switched one without any change to the wiring or fixing.

Switch off the power at the consumer unit and take out the circuit fuse or remove (or lock off) the MCB, then undo the fixing screws from the faceplate and pull the socket out of the box.

Loosen the terminals to free the conductors. Check that all is well inside the box, then connect the conductors to the terminals of the new socket. Fit the faceplate, using the original screws if those supplied with the new socket don't match the thread in the box.

Surface to flush

If you have to renew a surface-mounted socket for any reason, you may want to take the opportunity to replace it with a neater flush one.

Replacing a single socket with a double

One way to increase the number of socket outlets in a room is to substitute doubles for singles. Any single socket on a ring circuit can be replaced with a double without making any changes to the wiring.

A single socket on a spur can be replaced with a double one so long as it's the only socket on that spur – it needs to be connected to a single cable. To ensure that a socket fed by two cables is not one of two sockets on the same spur (which is no longer permitted), carry out the ring-circuit continuity test – see opposite.

Remember to switch off the power before making any alterations.

Surface to surface

Replacing a surface-mounted single socket with a surface-mounted double is easy.

Having removed the old socket outlet, simply fix the new, double box to the wall in the same place.

Flush to flush

Remove the old single socket and its metal box, then try the new double box over the hole. You can either centre the box over the hole or align it with one end, whichever is more convenient. Trace the outline of the box on the wall and cut out the brickwork.

Use a similar procedure to substitute a double socket for a single in a hollow wall, installing the socket by whichever method is most convenient.

Flush to surface

To avoid the disturbance to decor that is involved in installing a flush double socket, fit a special surface-mounted, pattress, which is made with two fixing holes that will line up with the fixing lugs on the buried metal box. You can use the blanked-off holes in the back of a standard plastic pattress for a similar purpose, but the special converter is much slimmer.

Surface to flush

To replace a single surface-mounted socket with a flush double, cut a recess for the metal box in the normal way.

Wiring a socket outlet

When a single cable is involved, strip off the sheathing in the normal way and connect the wires to the terminals: the blue wire to neutral – N; the brown one to live – L; and the earth wire, which you should insulate yourself with a sleeve, to earth – E (**1**). If necessary, fold the stripped ends over, so that no bare wire protrudes from a terminal.

Connecting to a ring-circuit cable
When connecting to a ring circuit, cut through the loop of cable and strip the sheathing from each half. Insert the bared ends of matching wires – live with live and so on – into the terminals (**2**). Slip sleeves onto the earth wires. After tightening the terminal screws, pull on each wire to ensure it is fixed securely.

Stiff cable can make it difficult to close the faceplate, so bend each conductor until it folds into the box. Locate the fixing screws and tighten them gradually in turn until the plate fits properly.

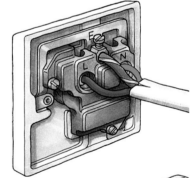

1 Wiring a socket outlet

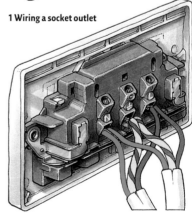

2 Connecting a socket to a ring circuit

Fixing a surface-mounted pattress over a flush box

SEE ALSO > Switching off 20, Stripping cable 26, Sockets 30, Mounting to a hollow wall 30–1, Recessing a mounting box 31

Adding a spur to a ring

If you need more socket outlets in a room, you can run 2.5mm² spur cables from a ring circuit and have as many unfused spurs as there are sockets or FCUs already on the ring. A spur can feed one single or one double socket.

A spur cable can be connected to any socket or fused connection unit on the ring circuit, or to a new junction box inserted in the circuit. If running a spur cable from an existing socket would mean disturbing the plaster, it will be more convenient to use a junction box; and if there is no socket outlet within easy reach of the proposed new one, using a junction box may save cable. If the cable is surface-run and you want to extend a row of sockets – behind a workbench, for example – then it will be simpler to connect the spur to a socket.

Examine the socket. If it is fed by a single cable, it is probably already on a spur; and if there are three cables in the socket, then it's already feeding a spur itself. What you need to look for is a socket that has two cables – but before you connect the spur to it, carry out a continuity test to make sure the socket is actually on a ring.

Testing for continuity

Isolate the ring circuit by switching off, then lock off the MCB or remove the fuse from the consumer unit. Unplug all appliances from the ring and switch off any fixed appliances connected to it.

Remove the socket, loosen the live terminal and separate the two red conductors. Leave the other wires in place. Using a multimeter set to its lowest resistance range, place one of the meter's probes on the socket's neutral terminal, and the other probe on the bared end of each red wire in turn. The meter reading should be high in each case.

Now touch one probe against the end of one of the red conductors, and the other probe against the end of the other red conductor. If the meter reading is low, you can be sure it is a ring circuit and you can safely add your spur.

Connecting to an existing socket

Fix the new socket, then wire it up in the normal way (see opposite) and run its spur cable to the existing socket outlet. Switch off the electricity and remove the existing socket. You may have to knock out another entry hole in order to feed the spur cable into the box. Prepare the conductors, and insert their bared ends together with those of the conductors of the ring circuit. Insert the wires in their terminals (brown/red – L; blue/black – N; and green-and-yellow – E). Replace the socket and switch the power on.

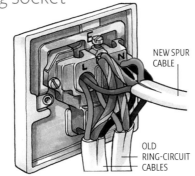

Taking a spur from an existing socket outlet

Using a junction box

You will need a 30amp junction box with three terminals to connect to a ring circuit. It will have either knock-out cable-entry holes or a special cover that rotates to blank off unneeded holes. Lift a floorboard close to the new socket, so you can connect to the ring-circuit cable without stretching it.

Making a platform

Make a platform for the box by screwing a 100 x 25mm (4 x 1in) strip of wood to battens fixed to the joists (see right). Loop the ring-circuit cable over the platform before fixing it, so that the cable need not be cut for connecting up. Remove the cover, screw the junction box to the platform, and break out three cable-entry holes. If you do forget to loop the cable over the platform, simply cut the cable when you come to connect it up.

Connecting the ring-circuit cable

Turn off the power at the consumer unit, then rest the ring-circuit cable across the box and mark the amount of sheathing to remove. Slit it lengthwise and peel it off the conductors. Don't cut the live and neutral conductors, but slice away just enough insulation on each to expose a section of bare wire that will fit into a terminal (see right). Cut the earth wire and fit insulating sleeves on the two ends.

Remove the screws from all three of the terminals and lay the wires across them – with the earth wire in the middle terminal. Push the wires home with a screwdriver.

Connecting the spur

Having fitted and wired the new spur socket, run its cable to the junction box. Prepare the ends of the spur wires and attach them to the terminals of the box (see right). Attach the new brown wire to the terminal holding the old red ones, and the new blue wire to the terminal holding the old black ones. Connect all earth wires to the central terminal. Replace the terminal screws. Check that all the wires are secured, with the sheathing running into the junction box, then fit the cover.

Fix each cable to a nearby joist with cable clips, to take the strain off the terminals, then replace the floorboards. Switch the power back on and test the new socket.

• **Old colour coding**
In a house built before 2005 you are likely to find that the existing cables are colour-coded black for neutral and red for live. The diagrams on this page show new-style spur cables being connected to old-style circuit cables.

Make a wooden platform for a junction box

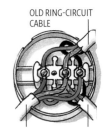

Taking a spur from a junction box

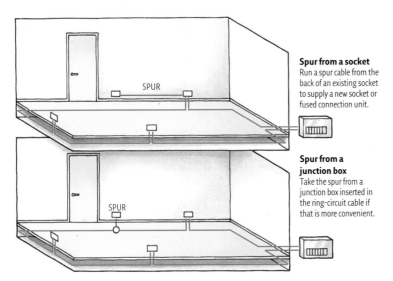

Spur from a socket
Run a spur cable from the back of an existing socket to supply a new socket or fused connection unit.

Spur from a junction box
Take the spur from a junction box inserted in the ring-circuit cable if that is more convenient.

SEE ALSO > Testing circuits 12–13, Switching off 20, Important notes at consumer unit 22, Cables 26, Stripping cable 26, Running cable 27–9

Fixed appliances

Socket outlets are designed to enable portable appliances to be moved from room to room, but many electrical appliances are fixed to the structure of the house or stand in one position all the time. Such appliances may therefore just as well be wired into your electrical installation permanently. Indeed in some cases there is no alternative, and some require radial circuits of their own direct from the consumer unit.

Fused connection units

A fused connection unit (FCU) is basically a device for joining the flex (or sometimes cable) of an appliance to circuit wiring. The connection unit incorporates the added protection of a cartridge fuse similar to that found in a 13amp plug. If the appliance is connected by a flex, choose a unit that has a cord outlet in the faceplate.

Some fused connection units are fitted with a switch, and some of these have a neon indicator that shows at a glance whether they are switched on. A switched connection unit allows you to isolate the appliance from the mains.

All fused connection units are single (there are no double versions available) and have square faceplates that fit metal boxes for flush mounting or standard surface-mounted plastic boxes.

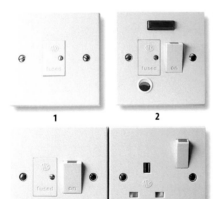

Fused connection units
1 Unswitched connection unit.
2 Switched unit with cord outlet and indicator.
3 Connection unit and socket outlet in a dual mounting box.

Mounting a fused connection unit

A fused connection unit is mounted in the same type of box as an ordinary socket outlet, and the box is fixed to the wall in exactly the same way. The unit can also be mounted in a dual box that is designed to hold two single units – for example, a standard socket outlet beside a connection unit. The socket is wired to the ring circuit, and the two units are linked together inside the box by a short 2.5mm² spur.

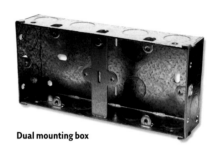

Dual mounting box

Wiring a fused connection unit

Before you wire a fused connection unit to the house circuitry, the power must be switched off at the consumer unit.

Fused connection units can be supplied by a ring circuit, a radial circuit or a spur. Some appliances are connected to the unit with flex, others with cable. Either way, the wiring arrangement inside the unit is the same. Units with cord outlets have clamps to secure the connecting flex.

An unswitched connection unit has two live (L) terminals – one marked 'Load' for the brown wire of the flex, and the other marked 'Mains' for the brown or red wire from the circuit cable. The blue wire from the flex and the blue or black wire from the circuit cable go to similar neutral (N) terminals; and both earth wires are connected to the unit's earth (E) terminal or terminals (**1**).

Switched connection units

A fused connection unit with a switch has two sets of terminals, too. Those marked 'Mains' are for the spur or ring cable that supplies the power; the terminals marked 'Load' are for the flex or cable from the appliance.

Wire up the flex side first, connecting the brown wire to the L terminal, and the blue one to the N terminal, both on the 'Load' side. Connect the green-and-yellow wire to the E terminal (**2**) and tighten the cord clamp.

Attach the circuit conductors to the 'Mains' terminals – brown or red to L, and blue or black to N; then sleeve the earth wire and take it to the E terminal (**2**).

If the fused connection unit is on a ring circuit, you need to fit two circuit conductors into each 'Mains' terminal and into the earth terminal.

Before screwing the unit to its box, make sure the wires are held firmly in the terminals and can fold away neatly.

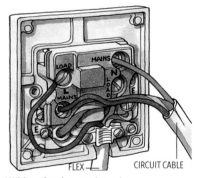

1 Wiring a fused connection unit

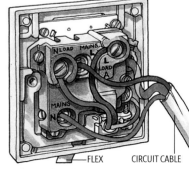

2 Wiring a switched fused connection unit

SEE ALSO > Stripping flex 17, Switching off 20, Power circuits 25, Stripping cable 26, Mounting boxes 30–1

Wiring small fixed appliances

Small permanent electrical appliances with ratings of up to 3000W (3kW) – wall heaters, extractor fans, cooker hoods and so on – can be wired into a ring or radial circuit by means of fused connection units. Although such appliances could be connected by means of 13amp plugs to socket outlets, the electrical contact would not be so good – and there is also some risk of fire with that type of permanent installation.

Flex outlets

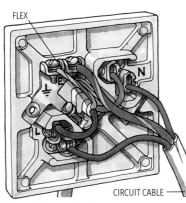

Flexible-cord outlet

In some situations, such as a bathroom, the fused connection unit has to be mounted in a different location from the appliance it is supplying with power.

If the appliance is fitted with flex, you can mount a flexible-cord outlet – 'flex outlet' next to the appliance – and then run a cable from the outlet to the FCU and connect it to the 'Load' terminals in the unit.

The flex outlet is mounted either on a standard surface-mounted box or flush on a metal box. At the back of the faceplate are three pairs of terminals to take the conductors from the flex and the cable.

N If you undertake work marked with this symbol, you must inform the BCO before starting – see FIRST THINGS FIRST.

FLEX

CIRCUIT CABLE

Wiring a flexible-cord outlet

Extractor fans **N**

To install a fan in a kitchen, mount a fused connection unit 150mm (6in) above the worktop. Run a cable to the fan or to a flexible-cord outlet next to it. If the fan has no integral switch, use a switched connection unit to control it. Fit a 3 or 5amp fuse, as recommended by the manufacturer.

If the fan's speed and direction are controllable, it may have a separate control unit – in which case you need to wire the connection unit to the control unit, following the manufacturer's instructions.

To install a fan in a bathroom, mount the fused connection unit outside the room and run the cable to the fan or flex outlet via a double-pole ceiling switch. The fan must be outside zones 0 and 1, and the circuit protected by a 30 milliamp RCD.

Wall-mounted fan
Run a 1.5mm² cable from a fused connection unit to a wall-mounted extractor fan.

Fridges, dishwashers and washing machines **N**

There is no reason why you cannot plug an appliance like a fridge, dishwasher or washing machine into a standard socket outlet – except that in a modern kitchen such appliances are installed under worktops, and sockets mounted behind them are difficult to reach. It's therefore generally more convenient to mount a switched fused connection unit 150mm (6in) above the worktop, then connect it to the ring circuit and run a spur – using 2.5mm² cable – from the connection unit to a socket outlet mounted behind the appliance.

Cooker hoods **N**

Either mount a fused connection unit, fitted with a 3amp fuse, close to the cooker hood or mount the connection unit 150mm (6in) above the worktop and then run a 1.5mm² cable from the unit to a flexible-cord outlet beside the hood.

Instantaneous water heaters **N**

To provide an on-the-spot supply of hot water, you can install an instantaneous water heater above a washbasin or sink. Join a 3kW model by heat-resistant flex to a switched fused connection unit mounted out of reach of water splashes from the basin or sink.

If the heater is for use in a bathroom, wire it via a flex outlet to a ceiling pull-switch and then to a fused connection unit outside the bathroom. Fit a 13amp fuse in the unit.

Wire a 7kW water heater in the same way as a shower. If it is situated in the kitchen, you can use a double-pole wall switch to control it.

Waste-disposal units **N**

A waste-disposal unit is housed in the cupboard unit below the sink. Mount a switched fused connection unit 150mm (6in) above a worktop near the sink, but well out of reach of small children and splashes from the sink. From the unit, run a 1.5mm² cable to a flex outlet next to the waste-disposal unit. Clearly label the connection unit 'waste disposal', to avoid accidents. Fit a 13amp fuse.

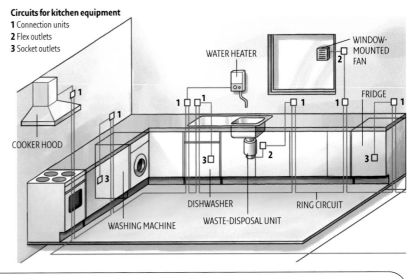

Circuits for kitchen equipment
1 Connection units
2 Flex outlets
3 Socket outlets

WINDOW-MOUNTED FAN
WATER HEATER
FRIDGE
COOKER HOOD
DISHWASHER
RING CIRCUIT
WASHING MACHINE
WASTE-DISPOSAL UNIT

SEE ALSO > Building Regulations 8, Bathroom safety 10, Zones for bathrooms 11, Switching off 20, Fuses 23, Running cable 27–9, Running a spur 33, Double-pole switches 40, Circuit lengths 68

Shaver sockets

N If you undertake work marked with this symbol, you must inform the BCO before starting – see FIRST THINGS FIRST.

Special shaver socket outlets are the only kind of electrical socket allowed in bathrooms. This type of socket contains a transformer that isolates the user side of the unit from the mains, reducing the risk of an electric shock.

This type of socket has to conform to the exacting British Standard BS EN 60742 Chapter 2, Section 1. However, there are shaver sockets that do not have an isolating transformer and therefore don't conform to this standard. These are safe to install and use in a bedroom – but must not be fitted in a bathroom.

• **RCD protection**
When installing any electrical appliance in a bathroom, the circuit must be protected by a 30 milliamp RCD.

Shaver unit for use in a bathroom

You can wire a shaver socket from a junction box on an earthed lighting circuit or from a fused connection unit, fitted with a 3amp fuse, on a ring-circuit spur. If you're installing the shaver socket in a bathroom, then the fused connection unit must be positioned outside the room. Run a 1.5mm² two-core-and-earth cable from the connection unit to the shaver socket; then connect the conductors: brown to L and blue to N. Sheathe the earth wire with a green-and-yellow sleeve and connect it to the earth (E) terminal.

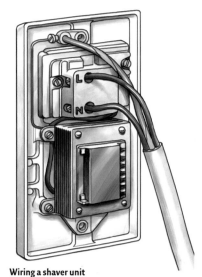
Wiring a shaver unit

Heated towel rails

When you're installing a heated towel rail in a bedroom, the appliance can be wired to a switched fused connection unit mounted next to the appliance, at a height of about 225 to 300mm (9in to 1ft) from the floor. For a towel rail of 1kW or less, fit a 5amp fuse in the connection unit; otherwise fit a 13amp fuse.

Heated towel rail in a bathroom
The Wiring Regulations covering other electrical equipment situated in bathrooms also apply to heated towel rails. The fused connection unit must be mounted outside the bathroom and wired to a convenient mains power circuit. Because the towel rail is mounted inside the bathroom, the circuit supplying power must be protected by a 30 milliamp RCD.

Run a spur cable from the fused connection unit to a flexible-cord outlet mounted beside the towel rail. Connect the cable's brown conductor to the flex outlet's live (L) terminal, and the blue conductor to the neutral (N) terminal.

Cover the bare copper earth wire with green-and-yellow sleeving and then attach it to the outlet's earth terminal.

Connect the flex from the towel rail similarly – brown conductor to live and blue to neutral. Connect the green-and-yellow-insulated earth conductor to the earth terminal.

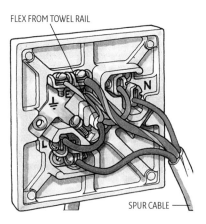
FLEX FROM TOWEL RAIL

SPUR CABLE

Wiring the flex outlet in a bathroom

Electric towel rail installed in a stylish modern bathroom

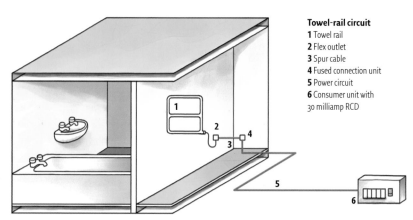

Towel-rail circuit
1 Towel rail
2 Flex outlet
3 Spur cable
4 Fused connection unit
5 Power circuit
6 Consumer unit with 30 milliamp RCD

SEE ALSO > Building Regulations 8, Bathroom safety 10, Zones for bathrooms 11, Switching off 20, Fuses 23, Running cable 27–9, Running a spur 33, Fused connection units 34, Flex outlets 35, Circuit lengths 68

Door bells and chimes

Whether you choose a door bell, a buzzer or a set of chimes, there are no practical differences that affect the way they are installed.

Wiring a bell push

Door bells
Most door bells are of the 'trembler' type. When electricity is supplied to the bell – that is when someone presses the button at the door – it activates an electromagnet, which causes a striker to hit the bell. But as the striker moves to the bell it breaks a contact, cutting off power to the magnet – so the striker swings back, makes contact again and repeats the process, going on for as long as the button is depressed. This type of bell can be operated by battery or (if it is an AC bell) by a mains transformer, which may be situated inside the unit or mounted separately.

Buzzers
A buzzer operates on exactly the same principle as a trembler bell, but in a buzzer the striker hits the magnet itself instead of a bell.

Chimes
A set of ordinary door chimes has two tubes or bars tuned to different notes. Between them is a solenoid, containing a spring-loaded plunger which acts like the trembler striker described above. Most

Wireless door chimes
You can continue using the socket even when a wireless door chime is plugged into it.

chimes can be run from a battery or transformer.

Bell pushes
Pressing a bell push completes the circuit that supplies power to the bell. The bell push is in effect a switch that is operated by holding it in the 'on' position. Inside it are two contacts, to which the circuit wires are connected. One contact is spring-loaded, touching the other when the button is depressed, to complete the circuit, and then springing back again when the button is released.

Illuminated bell pushes incorporate a tiny bulb, which enables you to see the bell push in the dark. These have to be operated from a mains transformer – as the power to the bulb, although only a trickle, is on continuously and would soon drain a battery. Luminous types glow at night without a power supply.

Wireless bell pushes
To remove the need for wiring, use a bell push that sends a radio signal to its bell. The bell can be moved around the house; and you can add a second bell, if required.

Batteries or transformer?

Some bells and chimes house batteries inside the casing, while other types incorporate a built-in transformer that reduces the 230V mains electricity to the very low voltages needed for this kind of equipment. For many door bells or chimes you can use either method. Most of them take either two, three or four 1½V batteries, but some need a 4½V battery that is housed separately.

The transformers sold for use with door-bell systems have three low-voltage

tappings (3V, 5V and 8V), to cater for various needs. Generally 3V and 5V connections are adequate for bells or buzzers; the 8V tapping is suitable for many sets of chimes.

However, some door chimes require a higher voltage, and for these you will need a transformer that has 4V, 8V and 12V tappings. A bell transformer must be designed in such a way that the full mains voltage cannot cross over to the low-voltage wiring.

Installing a system

The bell itself can be installed in any convenient position. Keep the bell-wire runs as short as possible, especially for a battery-operated bell. With a mains-powered bell you will want to avoid long runs of cable – so position the transformer where it can be wired simply. A cupboard under the stairs is usually a good place.

Drill a small hole in the doorframe and pass the bell wire through to the outside. Fix the conductors to the terminals of the bell push, then screw it over the hole.

If the battery is housed in the bell casing, there will be two terminals for attaching the other ends of the wires. Either wire can go to either terminal. If the battery is separate from the bell, run the bell wire from the push to the bell. Separate the conductors, cut one of them and join each cut end to a bell terminal. Run the wire on to the battery and attach it to the terminals.

Wiring to a transformer
If you are wiring to a transformer, proceed as above but connect the bell wire to whichever two of the three terminals combine to provide you with the necessary voltage. Some bells and chimes require separate lengths of bell wire, one from the bell push and another from the transformer. Fix the wires to terminals in the bell housing, following the maker's instructions.

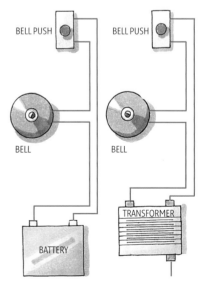

BELL PUSH BELL PUSH

BELL BELL

BATTERY TRANSFORMER

1 Battery circuit   **2 Transformer circuit**

Circuit wiring

The battery, bell push and bell are linked by two-core insulated 'bell wire'. This fine wire is usually surface-run, but can be run under floors. Bell wire is also used for connecting a bell and bell push to a transformer.

Connect a BS 3535 Part 2 double-insulated transformer to a junction box or ceiling rose on a lighting circuit with 1.5mm² two-core-and-earth cable. As no

earth is required for a double-insulated transformer, cut and tape back the earth wire at the transformer end. Or you can run a spur from a ring circuit in 2.5mm² two-core-and-earth cable to an unswitched fused connection unit, fitted with a 3amp fuse; then run a 1.5mm² two-core-and-earth cable from the connection unit to the transformer's 'Mains' terminals.

SEE ALSO > Switching off 20, Consumer units 22, Running cable 27–9, Running a spur 33, Fused connection units 34, Connection to a light circuit 55

Wiring a cooker

Appliances, such as cookers, that have a power load greater than 3000W (3kW) must have their own radial circuits connected directly to the consumer unit, with separate fuses protecting them.

Cooker circuits

Small table cookers and separate ovens that rate no more than 3kW can be connected to a ring circuit by a fused connection unit or even by means of a 13amp plug and socket. However, most cookers are much more powerful and must be installed on their own circuits.

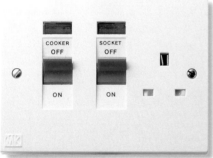
Cooker control unit with socket

Basic control unit

Terminal outlet box

The radial circuit

A cooker must be connected to a radial circuit – a single cable that runs back to the consumer unit. Between the cooker and the consumer unit, you must install a cooker control unit (which is basically a double-pole isolating switch). Some cooker control units incorporate a single 13amp socket outlet that can be used for appliances such as an electric kettle.

When cookers up to 13.5kW are connected to a control unit that has a socket, the radial circuit must be run using 4mm² two-core-and-earth cable and it must be protected by a 30amp fuse or a 32amp MCB. Larger cookers, up to 18kW, can be connected to a similar circuit, but you must use 6mm² two-core-and-earth cable and a 40amp MCB – you cannot use a fuse. (See CIRCUITS: MAXIMUM LENGTHS).

With either of the circuits described above, it's safe to use a unit that does not have a socket outlet. In fact, if you use a socketless unit, the Wiring Regulations allow you to run longer circuit lengths and to use a fuse with the larger cookers (instead of an MCB). If either of these is desirable, consult an electrician.

Connecting to the consumer unit

You can either use an existing fuseway that is already protecting a cooker circuit or, if there's an empty fuseway in your consumer unit, you can use this for the new cooker

circuit. If your consumer unit has fuses instead of MCBs, before installing the cooker circuit make sure they are cartridge fuses and not the rewirable type.

Positioning the cooker control unit

The control unit must be situated within 2m (6ft 6in) of the cooker. The unit must never be installed directly above a cooker, hob or oven, and it has to be easily accessible – so don't install the unit inside a cupboard or under a worktop.

A single control unit can serve both sections of a split-level cooker, with separate cables running to the hob and the oven, provided that the control unit is within 2m (6ft 6in) of both parts. (If this isn't possible with your cooker, you will need to install a separate control unit for each part.) The connecting cables must be of the same size as the cable used in the radial circuit. If the combined total of oven and hob exceeds 15kW, the circuits must be increased to 6mm² two-core-and-earth cable

A freestanding cooker will have to be moved from time to time for cleaning, so wire it with sufficient cable to allow it to be moved well out from the wall. The cable is connected to a terminal outlet box, which is screwed to the wall about 600mm (2ft) above floor level. A fixed cable runs from the outlet box to the cooker control unit.

Circuit for freestanding cooker
1 Cooker
2 Terminal outlet box
3 Control unit
4 Radial circuit
5 Consumer unit

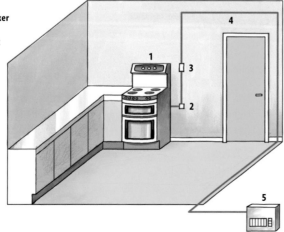

Circuit for separate hob and oven
1 Oven
2 Hob
3 Control unit
4 Radial circuit
5 Consumer unit

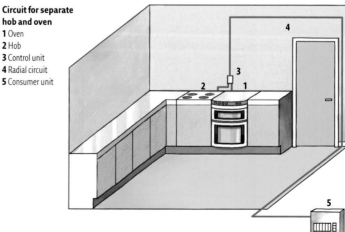

SEE ALSO > Consumer units 22, Circuit fuses 23, Circuit lengths 68

Wiring a freestanding cooker

Prepare a surface-mounted box for the cooker control unit by knocking out the cable-entry holes, and then screw it to the wall. If it's to be flush-mounted, cut a hole in the plaster and brickwork for a metal box. Cable-entry holes in metal boxes must be lined with blind grommets.

Running cable
Run the supply cable from the consumer unit, taking the most economical route to the cooker. If the cable is to be buried in the plaster, cut a vertical chase in the wall up to the cooker control unit, then cut a similar chase for the cable running to the terminal outlet box.

Connecting up the control unit
Feed the circuit cable and cooker cable into the control unit, then strip and prepare the conductors for connection.

There are two sets of terminals in the control unit: one marked 'Mains' for the circuit conductors, and the other marked 'Load' for the cooker cable. Run the brown wires to the L terminals, and the blue ones to the terminals marked N. Put green-and-yellow sleeves on both earth conductors and connect them to the E terminal (1). When all conductors are fixed securely, screw the faceplate to the mounting box.

1 Wiring the cooker control unit
The faceplate has to be removed in order to wire some cooker control units.

RADIAL-CIRCUIT CABLE
TOP
MAINS
L2
LOAD
E
EARTH
CABLE TO TERMINAL OUTLET BOX

Wiring the terminal outlet box
Run the cable down the wall from the cooker control unit to the terminal outlet box. This box has a set of terminals for connecting both cables – the one from the control unit and the other from the cooker itself.

Prepare the wires from both cables and insert them in the same terminals (2), matching colour for colour. Secure the sheathed part of both cables with the clamp, and then screw the plastic faceplate onto the outlet box.

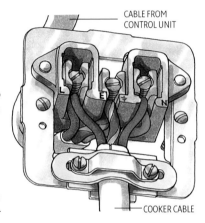

CABLE FROM CONTROL UNIT

COOKER CABLE

2 Wiring the terminal outlet box

Wiring the cooker
A panel on the back of the cooker has to be removed to gain access to the terminals. Prepare the end of the cable ready for connection, and release the cable clamp so that the cable can be slipped under it.

Undo the terminal nuts, so you can trap the bared end of each conductor under the terminal clamp; the brown cable conductor is connected to the live (L) terminal, and the blue conductor to the neutral (N) terminal (3); then tighten both terminal nuts. Sleeve the copper earth conductor and connect it to the earth (E) terminal.

Tighten the cable clamp and replace the back panel.

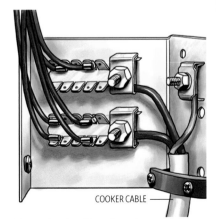

COOKER CABLE

3 Connecting the cable to the cooker terminals

Wiring a hob and oven

The procedure for wiring a separate hob and oven is similar to that described for a freestanding cooker, but because the appliances are fixed permanently in place there is no need to provide terminal outlet boxes. Instead, the cables running from the cooker control unit are wired directly to the hob and oven.

Connecting the cables
At the cooker control unit, connect the incoming radial-circuit cable to the 'Mains' terminal, as described far left.

Feed the cables from the appliances into the cooker control unit, then strip the conductors and prepare them for connection. Connect the bared ends of both brown conductors to the same live (L) terminal on the 'Load' side of the control unit. Similarly, insert both of the blue conductors together into the same neutral (N) terminal.

Cover the two earth conductors with green-and-yellow sleeving and then connect them to the common earth (E) terminal. Check that all conductors are fixed securely, before you screw the faceplate in place.

Connecting to hob and oven
Connect the hob and oven to their respective cables as described left.

N If you undertake work marked with this symbol, you must inform the BCO before starting – see FIRST THINGS FIRST.

At the consumer unit

Once you have tested the new radial circuit yourself, you can connect the prepared cable to the consumer unit.

With the main switch turned off, remove the fuse carrier or switch off the MCB. You must turn off the control unit and cooker controls, too.

Sheathe the incoming earth conductor in green-and-yellow sleeving and then connect it to a spare terminal in the earth block. Connect the blue conductor to a spare terminal in the neutral block. Finally, connect the brown conductor to the 'Load' terminal on the MCB or fuseway.

Having ruled out any obvious faults yourself, ask the BCO to carry out the necessary tests before you switch on and use the new circuit.

SEE ALSO > Building Regulations 8, Testing circuits 12–13, Consumer units 22, Stripping cable 26, Running cable 27–9, Flush mounting 31

Wiring a shower

An electrically heated shower unit is plumbed into the mains water supply. The flow of water operates a switch to energize an element that heats the water on its way to the shower sprayhead. Because there's so little time to heat the flowing water, instantaneous showers use a heavy load – from 6 to 10.8kW. Consequently, an electrically heated shower unit has to have a separate radial circuit, which must be protected by a 30 milliamp RCD. In addition, for showers up to 10.3kW the radial circuit must be protected by a 45amp MCB or fuse, either in a spare fuseway at the consumer unit or in a separate single-way consumer unit; a 10.8kW shower needs a 50amp MCB. The circuit cable needs to be 10mm² two-core-and-earth.

The shower unit itself has its own on/off switch, but there must also be a separate isolating switch in the circuit. This must not be accessible to anyone using the shower, so you need to install a ceiling-mounted 45amp double-pole pull-switch (a 50amp switch is required for a 10.8kW shower). The switch has to be fitted with an indicator that tells you when the switch is 'on'.

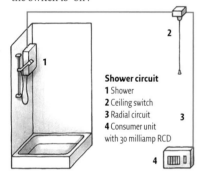

Shower circuit
1 Shower
2 Ceiling switch
3 Radial circuit
4 Consumer unit with 30 milliamp RCD

Connect the live and neutral conductors from the consumer unit to the switch's 'Mains' terminals, and those of the shower cable to the 'Load' terminals. Connect both earth wires, which have to be covered with green-and-yellow sleeving, to the single earth terminal on the switch.

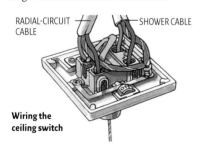

RADIAL-CIRCUIT CABLE

SHOWER CABLE

Wiring the ceiling switch

The shower unit itself must be wired according to the manufacturer's instructions. The unit and all metal pipes and fittings must be bonded to earth.

Immersion heaters

The water in a storage cylinder can be heated by an electric immersion heater, providing a central supply of hot water for the whole house. In many centrally heated homes the water is heated indirectly by the boiler, and an immersion heater is used as a backup for when the central heating has been switched off.

Types of immersion heater

1 Single element

2 Double element

3 Side-entry elements

An immersion heater can be installed either from the top of the cylinder or from the side, and top-entry units can have single or double elements.

With the single-element top-entry type, the element extends down almost to the bottom of the cylinder, so that all of the water is heated whenever the heater is switched on (**1**).

For economy, one of the elements in the double-element type is a short one for top-up heating, while the other is a full-length element that heats the entire contents of the cylinder (**2**). A double-element heater that has a single thermostat is called a twin-element heater; one with a thermostat for each element is known as a dual-element heater.

Side-entry elements are of identical length. One is positioned near to the bottom of the cylinder, and the other a little above halfway up (**3**).

Adjusting the water temperature
The thermostat that controls the maximum temperature of the water is set by adjusting a screw inside the cap covering the terminal box.

Adjusting the thermostat

Heating water on the night rate

If you have storage heaters, your electricity company supplies you with cheap-rate power for seven hours sometime between midnight and 8.00 a.m., the exact period being at the discretion of the company. This scheme is called Economy 7.

If you have a cylinder that is large enough to store hot water for a day's requirements, you can benefit by heating all your water during the Economy 7 hours. For the water to retain its heat all day, the cylinder must be insulated.

If your cylinder is already fitted with an immersion heater, you can use the existing wiring by fitting an Economy 7 programmer, a device that will switch your immersion heater on at night and heat up the whole cylinder. Then if you run out of hot water during the day, you can always adjust the programmer's controls to boost the temperature briefly. You can make even greater savings if you have two side-entry immersion heaters or a dual-element one. The programmer will switch on the longer element, or the

bottom one, at night; if the water needs heating during the day, then the upper or shorter element is used.

Economy 7 without a programmer
You can have a similar setup without a programmer if you wire two separate circuits for the elements. The upper element is wired to the daytime supply, while the lower one is wired to its own switchfuse unit and operated by the Economy 7 time switch during the hours of the night-time tariff only. A setting of 75°C (167°F) is recommended for the lower element, and 60°C (140°F) for the upper one. If your water is soft or your heater elements are sheathed in titanium or incoloy, you can raise the temperatures to 80°C (175°F) and 65°C (150°F) respectively without unduly reducing the life of the elements.

Leave the upper unit switched on permanently. It will only heat up if the thermostat detects a temperature of 60°C (140°F) or less, which should happen rarely if the cylinder is properly insulated.

SEE ALSO > Reducing electricity bills 6–7, Building Regulations 8, Bonding to earth 10, Zones for bathrooms 11, Consumer units 22, Circuit fuses 23, Running cable 27–9, Circuit lengths 68

The circuit

The majority of immersion heaters are rated at 3kW; but although you can wire most 3kW appliances to a ring circuit, an immersion heater is regarded as using 3kW continuously, even though rarely switched on all the time. A continuous 3kW load would seriously reduce a ring circuit's capacity, so immersion heaters must have their own radial circuits.

The circuit needs to be run in 2.5mm² two-core-and-earth cable protected by a 15amp fuse or 16amp MCB. Each element must have a special double-pole isolating switch mounted near the cylinder; the switch should be marked 'water heater' and have a neon indicator. A 2.5mm² heat-resistant flexible cord runs from the switch to the immersion heater.

If the cylinder is situated in a bathroom, the switch must be outside zones 0 to 2. If this precludes a standard water-heater switch, fit a 20amp ceiling-mounted pull-switch with a mechanical on/off indicator. When installing any electrical appliance in a bathroom, the circuit must be protected by a 30 milliamp RCD.

Heater circuit
1 Heater
2 Flex
3 Switch
4 Radial circuit
5 Consumer unit

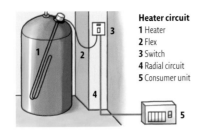

20amp switch for an immersion heater

If you undertake work marked with this symbol, you must inform the BCO before starting – see FIRST THINGS FIRST.

Wiring the switch and heater

Feed the circuit cable into the switch mounting box fixed to the wall, and connect it to the 'Mains' terminals – brown to L, blue to N. Sheathe the earth wire in a green-and-yellow sleeve, then connect it to the common earth terminal (1). Prepare a heat-resistant flex for the switch. Connect the green-and-yellow earth wire to the common earth terminal and the other wires to the 'Load' terminals – brown to L, and blue to N. Tighten the flex clamp before screwing the switch faceplate in place.

The flex from the switch goes to the heater. Feed it through the hole in the cap, and then prepare the wires for connection.

Connect the brown flex wire to one of the terminals on the thermostat (the other one is already connected to the

wire running to the live terminal on the heating element). Connect the blue wire to the neutral terminal, and the green-and-yellow wire to the earth terminal (2). Replace the cap, which covers all the heater terminals and the thermostat.

Connecting to the consumer unit

Run the circuit cable from the cylinder cupboard to the fuse board. With the power switched off, connect the cable to an empty fuseway in the consumer unit (see WIRING A COOKER). Although the consumer unit is switched off, the cable between the main switch and the meter will remain live – so take special care.

Having ruled out any obvious faults yourself, ask the BCO to carry out the necessary tests before you switch on and use the new circuit.

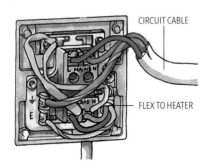
CIRCUIT CABLE
FLEX TO HEATER
1 Wiring the switch

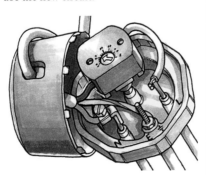
2 Wiring the heater

Replacing an element

With time, immersion heaters simply burn out and you are left without hot water. You can replace a heater yourself without notifying your BCO. First, check the circuit fuse or MCB; and if that isn't the source of the problem, isolate the heater circuit at the consumer unit and turn off the switch beside the cylinder. If your water is also heated by a boiler, switch that off, too.

Testing the immersion heater

Take the cap off the heater and, to test that the power has been switched off, touch the neutral terminal with one probe of a mains-voltage tester and the incoming live terminal on the thermostat with the other probe (1). Now do the same between incoming live terminal and the earth. If the power is off, make a note of the way the wires are connected to the heater, then disconnect the flex.

To check for a faulty thermostat, set it for maximum temperature and, using a multimeter set to its lowest resistance range, place one of the meter's probes on each of the thermostat terminals (2). If the meter shows no continuity, you only need to replace the thermostat – which saves having to drain the cylinder. If the thermostat seems to be functioning, place the probes on the heater terminals (3); and if there is no continuity, replace the heater.

Replacing the heater

To buy a replacement, estimate the diameter of the cylinder or the length of a top-entry heater. Heaters are usually supplied with the thermostat ready-fitted. You will also need to buy either an immersion-heater ring spanner or a special box spanner for turning an element surrounded by foam insulation.

Before you drain the cylinder, turn the heater very slightly with the spanner to free the threads (4). Now drain the cylinder, unscrew the heater and lift it out.

Fit the large washer supplied with the new heater, then screw the heater in place by hand until you feel the threads turning smoothly. The washer should prevent any leaks, but you can wrap PTFE tape around the heater threads as an extra precaution. Never smear it with sealant. Give a final turn with the spanner to tighten the heater, but don't apply too much force or you could distort the thin metal of the cylinder.

With the help of your notes, replace the wires on their terminals as they were on the old element (5); and then set the thermostat to the required temperature (see opposite). Replace the cap, refill the cylinder and check for leaks; then restore the power.

1 Check that the power is off

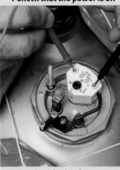
2 Test for a faulty thermostat

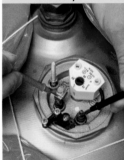
3 Test the heater

4 Free the heater threads

5 Replace the wires

SEE ALSO > Building Regulations 8, Zones for bathrooms 11, Testing circuits 12–13, Connecting flex 17, Stripping cable 26, Running cable 27–9, Switching off 20, Consumer units 22, Circuit lengths 68

Communication equipment

The modern British home is equipped with all manner of communication equipment, including telephones, computers, television sets and digital radios. No one but an expert would be advised to try to make major repairs to these appliances, but there's a lot you can do to boost their performance and to make using them more convenient.

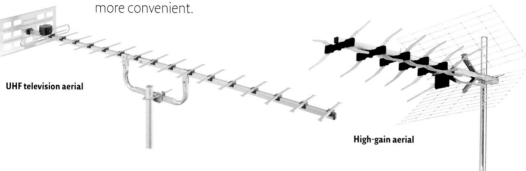

UHF television aerial

High-gain aerial

Television sets and aerials

The television set is probably the most widely used electronic appliance in the home, with most households boasting two or more large-screen or portable sets. This dependence on TV is becoming costly in terms of energy, with the larger plasma-screen sets consuming up to four times more power than the average television. The situation is greatly magnified by all the peripheral equipment, such as DVD players and recorders, especially when appliances are left on standby.

In Britain, the transmission of analogue TV signals is in the process of being phased out in favour of digital signals. However, at the moment our TV pictures and sound are broadcast in analogue format from about 1000 transmitters. Only a small percentage are high-power main transmitters, the majority being smaller low-power transmitters designed to relay the signals to homes outside the scope of the main transmitters. In order to receive these signals, a TV set must be connected to a suitable aerial.

Outdoor aerial
TV aerials erected outside usually provide better reception than a similar aerial mounted in the loft.

Outdoor aerials

Aerials mounted on the roof or clamped to a tall mast afford the best possible reception. An outdoor aerial can be installed in the loft, but – depending on the strength of the broadcast signal – picture quality may be reduced.

This type of aerial has a number of elements (crosspieces) and, as a rule, the more elements there are the better the reception. If you happen to live in an area where the incoming signal is weak, you may benefit from using a high-gain aerial, with an even greater number of elements designed to gather more of the available signal.

When directed towards a mains transmitter, an aerial should be mounted with its elements parallel to the ground. If it is receiving a signal from a relay transmitter, then the elements should be vertical.

Indoor aerials

If it's not possible to connect your TV set to an outdoor aerial, a good-quality set-top aerial may be the best solution. There are directional indoor aerials – which work best when aimed at the transmitter. Omnidirectional aerials are designed to receive signals from any angle, but in practice you may still have to try the aerial in different positions to get the best reception.

Digital terrestrial broadcasting

By converting TV pictures and sound into binary code, digital broadcasters can transmit much more information than is possible with the analogue format. As a result, there are several advantages to be gained from a digital system:

- Sharp, clear pictures with CD-quality sound.
- Greater choice of programmes.
- Greatly enhanced Teletext service.
- Interactive TV.

Because the majority of terrestrial broadcasting operates on the same frequencies as analogue television, many households can continue using their existing outdoor aerials. However, the aerial may have to be realigned and, in some areas, a new wideband UHF aerial may be required.

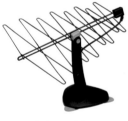

Indoor aerial

Regardless of the aerial you use, in order to receive digital broadcasts you will either have to install a set-top box to decode the signals or buy a digital TV set with an integral decoder.

Digital radio

Digital Audio Broadcasting (DAB) converts sound into binary code. The benefits over FM and AM transmissions include almost CD-quality sound and interference-free reception.

To receive digital radio broadcasts, you require a digital receiver. If you need a separate aerial, a VHF aerial that covers Band 3 between 211.5 and 230MHz is usually recommended. Before you spend a lot of money on equipment, ask around to see what the reception is like in your area – with digital radio you invariably get an error-free signal or nothing at all.

Satellite broadcasting

Satellite broadcasters transmit low-power signals to a satellite in a geostationary orbit above the earth. The satellite amplifies the signals, converts them to a different frequency and transmits them back to earth. Signal strength is also affected by weather conditions, with cloud cover, rain and snow all tending to degrade quality of reception.

To receive a satellite signal, you need a dish of a suitable size and shape. As a rule, the weaker the signal the larger the dish required in order to receive acceptable pictures and sound. Large dishes, which have relatively narrow angles of reception, concentrate the signal and reduce interference but require more accurate alignment.

The low-noise block suspended in front of the dish reduces the signals to a lower frequency and sends them via a coaxial

SEE ALSO > Installing aerial sockets 44

cable to the satellite receiver – this is the unit that converts the signals into a format that can be displayed on the television screen.

Digital satellite broadcasting

A digital satellite broadcaster can transmit literally hundreds of channels, with a mixture of subscription and pay-as-you-view services. To receive digital satellite broadcasts, you need the appropriate set-top decoder or a TV set with an integral decoder, and you will probably have to get a smaller digital dish aerial. If you want to receive both analogue and digital transmissions, you will need two satellite dishes.

Installing a dish

Installing your own dish aerial is a simple DIY project, but it involves altering the direction of the aerial to obtain the strongest signal. In practice, this is probably best left to the TV supplier or satellite station, who usually offer free installation as part of the package.

Have a satellite dish installed by a professional

Cable TV

TV signals delivered by underground cables are not as susceptible to the sorts of interference that affect ordinary satellite reception. To receive them, you need the appropriate set-top or integral decoders – similar to but different from those required for satellite broadcasting.

Other services

Cable-TV suppliers can also provide broadband connection for your computer and an independent dedicated phone line. Installation is not a DIY job and the cable provider will make all the necessary connections and adjustments. It's worth asking your installer whether it is possible to avoid unsightly surface wiring, but be prepared to do some of the preparatory work yourself.

Signal boosters

In locations where the TV or FM radio signals are weak, a signal booster (amplifier) will improve reception appreciably. With the appropriate booster, you can distribute the signals to a number of TV sets and audio systems without loss of quality.

Masthead amplifiers

In areas where reception is particularly poor, it would be worth having a high-gain outdoor aerial connected to a masthead signal amplifier. Mounted outside, the amplifier is powered by a special power-supply unit, which is plugged into an indoor wall socket.

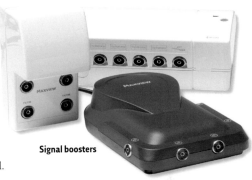

Signal boosters

If you ask the installer to fit a 'diplexer' alongside the amplifier, you can gather and distribute signals from both a TV aerial and an FM radio aerial.

Masthead signal amplifier
1 High-gain outdoor aerial
2 Signal amplifier
3 Wall socket
4 Power-supply unit
5 Coaxial cable
6 Television set

Plug-in signal boosters

For best-quality reception a signal booster should be placed as close to the aerial as possible – but for sheer convenience it's hard to beat a booster that you simply plug into a socket next to the television set. Having plugged the incoming aerial cable into the booster, you can then connect up as many appliances as the booster is designed to accommodate.

Other signal boosters are fitted with a 13amp plug on the end of a short length of flex. This type can be left freestanding on a shelf close to your TV set and hi-fi system, or you can mount it on the wall. Some of these are 'fixed-gain' boosters, and some are made with a dial or switch that allows you to increase and decrease the signal gain as required.

Some indoor TV aerials are made with integral signal boosters.

Installing a booster

It's advisable to get a professional to put up a masthead amplifier, but you can install a booster yourself indoors. To fit a typical fixed-gain signal booster, screw the mounting box supplied with the booster to the wall or skirting board (**1**). Check that it's level before tightening the screws.

Connect the coaxial cables from your television sets and audio system, and also the aerial cable (**2**).

Screw the booster to the mounting box (**3**), then plug it into a 13amp wall socket and switch on.

1 Screw the mounting box to the wall

2 Plug in the aerial and the cables to your TV sets

3 Attach the booster to its mounting box

SEE ALSO > Wiring coaxial plugs 44

Installing aerial sockets

If you can't get satisfactory reception on every television set in your home, consider hooking all of them up to the main outdoor aerial. There are several ways to do this – including using a plug-in signal booster (already described). Another solution is to use surface-mounted aerial sockets to connect two TV sets to the same aerial.

Extending a TV aerial
1 Outdoor aerial
2 Splitter socket
3 Main TV set
4 Single aerial socket
5 Coaxial cable
6 Portable TV set

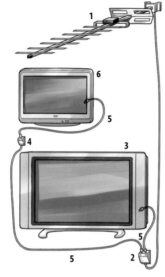

1 Mount the splitter socket

2 Remove the inner insulation

3 Clamp the braided copper

4 Connect to the splitter socket

5 Plug in the cables

Extending a TV aerial

Using a bradawl, make holes for screwing a splitter socket to the skirting close to your main TV set (**1**). Do the same for a single aerial socket in a similar position in the room where you use your second set.

Cut a length of coaxial cable to run from one socket to the other. Attach this cable to skirting boards and architraves, using cable clips. Alternatively, run the coaxial cable under the floor or inside hollow walls – but not next to mains electricity cables.

At the single socket, strip about 18mm (¾in) of sheathing from the cable, fold back the copper strands and then remove about 16mm (⅝in) of insulation to reveal the inner conductor (**2**). Using the socket as a guide, trim the solid conductor to length.

Connect the conductor to the terminal in the socket and trap the braided copper and sheathing under the cable clamp (**3**). Tighten both screws, then screw the socket to the skirting. Fit a coaxial plug (see right) to the other end of the cable, ready for plugging into the splitter.

Remove the coaxial plug from the end of the existing incoming aerial cable and then connect the cable to the splitter socket (**4**), as described above. Screw the socket in place.

Plug in the new cable running from the single socket (**5**). Make or buy two coaxial (RF) leads for your TV sets and connect them, one from each box, to the 'antenna in' (ANT) socket on the back of each set.

Wiring coaxial plugs

A special insulated and shielded (coaxial) cable is required to pass the incoming signals to your TV sets. There are several types, but most electrical outlets stock the common 6mm (¼in) low-loss cable. Coaxial cable is either wired directly into the back of aerial sockets or fitted with single-pin coaxial plugs for insertion into the sockets. The ones shown here are solderless fittings made with simple screw fixings.

Cut the cable to length and slide the plug's locking ring onto one end. Strip off about 30mm (1¼in) of the outer sheathing, taking care not to sever the fine copper strands in the process (**1**).

Unravel the copper strands and fold them back over the sheathing. Wind the strands in a clockwise direction until they cover the first 6mm (¼in) of the sheathing (**2**).

Slide the cable gripper onto the end of the

sheathing so that it covers the copper strands (**3**). Pinch the gripper onto the sheathing to contain the fine copper strands.

Strip all but about 3mm (⅛in) of the polythene insulation to reveal the solid copper conductor inside. Trim off excess conductor, leaving about 6mm (¼in) protruding from the insulation (**4**).

Loosen the fixing screw and insert the conductor into the plug's pin. Tighten the screw to secure the conductor (**5**).

Assemble the plug (**6**), making sure that none of the copper strands touch the inner conductor, then secure the fitting with the locking ring. Fit a similar plug to the other end of the cable.

1 Strip the sheathing to reveal the copper strands

2 Wind the strands around the sheathing

3 Slide the gripper over the strands

4 Trim the solid conductor to length

5 Clamp the conductor by tightening the screw

6 Assemble the coaxial plug

SEE ALSO > TV sets and aerials 42, Signal boosters 43

Telephone extensions

Although a telephone company must be employed to install the master socket that's connected to the incoming network cable, you are permitted to install extension cables and sockets yourself. All the necessary equipment is available from DIY outlets and from electronics stores and telephone shops.

Sockets and accessories
1 Single-socket faceplate
2 Surface-mounted socket
3 Socket doubler
4 Converter plug
5 British Telecom Linebox
6 Insertion tool

You can install as many telephone extension sockets as you want, so long as the total 'Ringer Equivalence Number' (REN) in your home does not exceed four. A telephone is normally allocated an REN of one – but it is advisable to check this before you decide which equipment to purchase. Telephones are made with either 'tone' or 'pulse' dialling, and modern phones can be switched from one to the other. The type of dialling does not affect the wiring of sockets.

Telephone sockets

The single and double sockets that accept the small rectangular telephone plugs are made in the form of square faceplates (**1**) that fit standard electrical metal and plastic mounting boxes. Compact surface-mounted sockets are also available (**2**).

To operate two telephones or a telephone and an answering machine from a single socket without additional wiring, simply plug in a socket doubler (**3**).

You can run an extension from any master socket by means of a converter plug (**4**), which usually comes complete with several metres of cable. Another option is to wire your extension cable directly into a British Telecom Linebox (**5**), which has a removable cover for customer access.

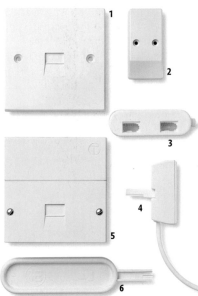

Running the circuit

Run a length of cable from the existing master socket to each extension socket. The cable can be pinned to the top of skirtings or along picture rails and doorframes, using small plastic cable clips. Alternatively, you can conceal the cable under the floorboards or within walls, provided it does not follow exactly the same route used for mains wiring – maintain a minimum of 75mm (3in) between the telephone cable and mains cables. At each socket, feed a loop of cable into the mounting box, ready for connection.

Connecting cable to blade terminals

Connecting to the sockets

At each socket, cut the loop of cable and strip the sheathing to expose the colour-coded conductors, then separate the conductors and connect them to the appropriate numbered terminals.

Telephone-socket terminals usually comprise two opposing brass blades that cut into the cable's insulation and make contact with the wire core as the conductor is forced between them with an insertion tool. Lay the insulated conductor across its terminal and press it firmly to the base of the terminal. Trim the end of the wire.

Other sockets are made with screw terminals. Strip about 6mm (¼in) of insulation from the end of each of the conductors, then insert the wire into the terminal and tighten the screw.

Sometimes, plastic cable ties are provided to secure the cable inside the socket, in order to prevent strain on the connections.

Inserting wires into screw terminals

Telephone cable

Telephones, including extensions, are wired with extra-low-voltage cable.

Telephone cable usually comprises six colour-coded conductors sheathed in PVC. However, four-core cable is often sold for running domestic telephone extensions, and is perfectly adequate provided you match the colour-coded conductors to any existing wiring (see chart below).

Socket terminals are numbered 1 to 6. Always match the same colour coding to the same number terminal in each socket. If you are using four-core cable, ignore terminals 1 and 6.

Number	Colour coding
Terminal 1	Green with white rings
Terminal 2	Blue with white rings
Terminal 3	Orange with white rings
Terminal 4	White with orange rings
Terminal 5	White with blue rings
Terminal 6	White with green rings

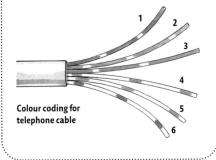

Colour coding for telephone cable

Wiring the master socket

Plugging a converter plug into the master socket will connect all your extensions to the telephone company network. To connect cable to a British Telecom Linebox, remove the front cover and use the insertion tool to introduce the conductors into the bladed terminals, as described left.

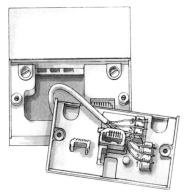

Connecting to a British Telecom Linebox

SEE ALSO > Running cable 27–9, Mounting boxes 30–1

An office at home

Working from home has become a practical option for a great many people. And even those who commute to the workplace usually need somewhere at home where they can catch up with extra work and sort out domestic accounts. Homework and hobbies place younger members of the family in a similar position. Increasingly, these activities are centred on a computer and a network of electronic equipment.

Whether you make do with a corner of the dining table or have the luxury of a dedicated workspace, some planning – and perhaps new wiring – will avoid a tangle of trailing flexes and overloaded socket outlets. To assess the number and positions of socket outlets, first plan your office layout to make the best use of the space available. Think about where your desk or worktable should be placed. You will probably want to take advantage of natural light – but before you make any permanent alterations, try out the position of your computer monitor to avoid distracting reflections from windows and fixed lighting.

Comfortable worktop
A desk with an adjustable worktop gives you the opportunity to have your keyboard at exactly the right height for comfort.

A worktop for your computer

Most people can work comfortably on a worktop that is 700mm (2ft 4in) from the floor. Ideally a computer keyboard should be slightly lower – which is why ready-made computer work stations are usually made with a slide-out work surface that can be stowed beneath the monitor. If your children are likely to use the same workspace, get a chair that is adjustable in height.

A fixed worktop needs to be at least 600mm (2ft) deep to provide enough room for the average computer and keyboard. But you may need a worktop 750mm (2ft 6in) deep to accommodate larger equipment, unless you can build an L-shape unit that allows the monitor, to be tucked into the corner.

Improved memory and screen quality has made the laptop computer a viable space saver for the home office.

Whatever computer you use, remember to provide extra worktop space for papers and reference books, plus shelves or drawers to store items such as stationery and computer disks.

Ancillary equipment

Even the most sophisticated computer is of limited use without a printer for accounts and correspondence, and to print out e-mails and downloads from the Internet. And you may want a scanner for putting your own photos and graphics onto the computer, which allows you to manipulate and recompose the images.

And as time goes by, you may require extra memory for data storage, which might mean a second hard drive for the computer. Handy USB memory sticks are a viable alternative, but they should not be relied upon for long-term storage.

Most offices are equipped with a paper shredder. Reduce the amount of paper you need to store by scanning documents onto your computer, then shred the paper.

The cable jungle

Each new piece of equipment needs a power supply and a connection to the computer – which is why so many home offices end up with a tangle of wires and overloaded sockets. You can tidy the cable runs with various cable ties and hoses, but having enough sockets positioned where needed is a better long-term solution.

Having to disconnect one appliance in order to use another is very inconvenient. Try connecting all your equipment to a USB hub plugged into the back of the computer.

A computer with wireless connection for e-mail and Internet downloads could help eliminate some cables.

Networking

If you have more than one computer, networking allows you to transfer data from one to the other. Similarly, printers and scanners can be shared. A network can be hard-wired, using Ethernet cables laid like ordinary mains cabling, but most people find a wireless network more convenient. For this, you will need a wireless router connected to the incoming Internet cable and to one of the computers. Any other computer can be connected by wireless receiver units, which plug into a USB socket or memory-card slot.

Lighting your office
Use dedicated task lighting to illuminate the work area without creating distracting reflections. A portable desk lamp is one option, or you could install a small spotlight or downlighter above the work station. A dimmer switch that controls the room lighting will allow you to set the optimum level of background illumination.

USB hub
A small USB hub allows you to connect several pieces of equipment to a single port on the back of your computer.

SEE ALSO > Light fittings 50–1

Providing extra sockets

Most householders just don't have the space to dedicate a room exclusively to working at home – but even if your study has to double as a spare bedroom from time to time, adding socket outlets will provide flexibility in the way you use your office or study and allow the room to be used for hobbies and games without compromising other activities.

Incorporate new socket outlets by adding spurs or extending the ring circuit. You will then be able to plug in as many appliances as you wish, including electric heaters, without fear of overloading the circuit. In addition, it will reduce the risk of a plug being pulled out accidentally, which could result in the loss of irreplaceable data.

Extending a ring circuit

With the power turned off, you can break into the ring circuit and connect a new length of cable, either to the existing sockets or by means of junction boxes. Sockets are relatively cheap – so be generous with the number you install and make sure you provide enough for all the equipment you are likely to need.

You'll probably need one or two extra socket outlets at skirting level, and two or three more at desktop height. This arrangement will provide you with the most direct route for connecting floor-standing and desktop equipment, without having to extend flexible cords. Where possible, rewire plugs – making the flex as short as practicable.

Label all the plugs that are connected to vulnerable equipment – including your computer. This simple precaution will reduce the risk of the equipment being unplugged inadvertently by another member of your family who wants to use the socket for another appliance.

Adding sockets
You could extend the ring circuit to add extra sockets at skirting level and to provide a source of power at desktop height.

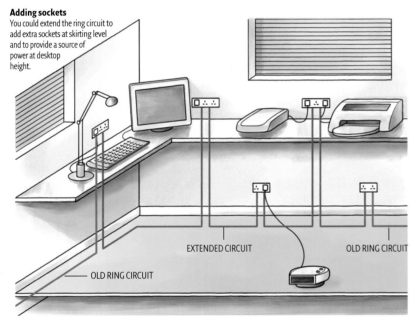

OLD RING CIRCUIT
EXTENDED CIRCUIT   OLD RING CIRCUIT

Telephones and modems

Unless your equipment utilizes wireless technology, you will need a telephone socket near your computer in order to access the Internet. To make better use of a single telephone socket, you can plug your phone and modem leads into a socket doubler.

British Telecom or similar telephone companies can advise you on broadband connection via the phone line or a network cable in order to receive faster downloads. This has the advantage of being able to use a single phone line for simultaneous phone and Internet use. If you use the phone a great deal, a 'voice over Internet'

connection might save you money.

Most people use an answerphone to pick up messages when they're not at home or are unavailable. These need to be connected to a telephone socket, and to a power supply via a 13amp plug. It is worth labelling this plug, in order to avoid accidental disconnection and the subsequent inconvenience of having to reprogram the unit.

If you don't have a dedicated photo-copier, you can equip your home office with a multipurpose printer/copier/fax machine or printer/copier/scanner, which are now relatively inexpensive.

Multi-way sockets

If extending your ring circuit is not a viable option, there are various ways of connecting more than one appliance to existing sockets outlets.

Trailing sockets

Trailing sockets are made with up to ten 13amp socket outlets, connected via a relatively short flexible lead to a single plug. With this type of device you can connect your computer and ancillary equipment to a single wall-mounted socket.

Look for trailing sockets fitted with surge suppressors (see right).

Surge protection
Sensitive electronic components in a computer can be damaged by voltage 'spikes' – short-duration peaks of high voltage. You can buy special plugs and trailing sockets fitted with surge suppressors designed to protect vulnerable equipment.

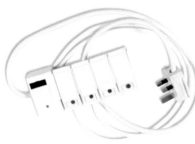

Miniature trailing sockets

There are special trailing sockets made with miniature plugs. They can be screwed to a skirting, or to the wall behind your desktop. There is one disadvantage with this equipment. Because the miniature plugs are not fused individually, a fault in any of the appliances connected to the trailing socket will cause the fuse in the 13amp plug to blow, and all of the appliances – including your computer – will be disconnected instantly. To protect vital data, have your computer plugged into its own wall socket and use the trailing socket for ancillary equipment only.

Wiring a miniature plug

Multi-adaptor

You can wire up to four appliances directly to a multi-adaptor, which has a short flex and 13amp plug for connecting to a single wall socket. The flex from each appliance is wired to its own set of terminals inside the adaptor, where it is protected by an individual fuse. Consequently, a fault on a single appliance is less likely to affect other equipment connected to the adaptor.

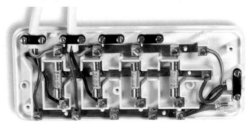

Each appliance is wired to a set of terminals

SEE ALSO > Switching off 20, Cables 26, Running cable 27–9, Sockets 30–2, Adding a spur 33

Lighting circuits

Every lighting system needs a feed cable to supply power to the various lighting points, and a switch that can interrupt the supply to each point. There are two ways of meeting these requirements in your home: the junction-box system and the loop-in system. Your house may be wired with either one, though it's quite likely that there will be a combination of the two systems.

Domestic systems

The junction-box system
With a junction-box system, the feed cable runs from the consumer unit to a series of junction boxes, one for each lighting point. From each box a separate cable runs to the light itself, and another runs to its switch.

The loop-in system
With the loop-in system, the ceiling rose takes the place of the junction box. The cable from the consumer unit runs into each rose and out again, then on to the next. The switch cable and the flex to the bulb are connected at the rose.

Combined system
The loop-in system is now more widely used since it entails fewer connections. However, lights located at some distance from a loop-in circuit are often run from a junction box on the circuit; and lights

added after the circuit has been installed are also often wired from junction boxes.

The circuits
Both the junction-box system and the loop-in system are, in effect, multi-outlet radial circuits. The cable runs from the consumer unit, looping in and out of the ceiling roses or junction boxes, and terminates at the last one. Unlike the cable of a ring circuit, it doesn't return to the consumer unit.

Lighting circuits require 1.5mm² two-core-and-earth cable, and each circuit needs to be protected by a 5amp circuit fuse or 6amp MCB in the consumer unit. A maximum of eleven 100W bulbs or their equivalent can therefore use the circuit.

In the average two-storey house the usual practice is to have two separate lighting circuits – one for the ground floor and the other for upstairs.

• No earth wires
If you uncover an old lighting system that lacks earth wires, reconnect the other wires temporarily and get expert advice on rewiring the circuit.

Detachable ceiling rose
If you use a modern detachable ceiling rose, you can slide out the centre section to change the light fitting without disturbing the fixed wiring. This type of rose can support a light fitting weighing up to 5kg (11lb).

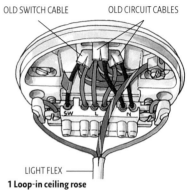

1 Loop-in ceiling rose

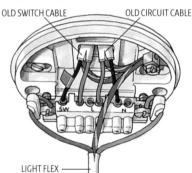

2 Last rose on a loop-in system

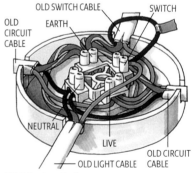

3 Lighting junction box

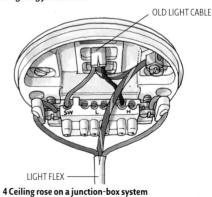

4 Ceiling rose on a junction-box system

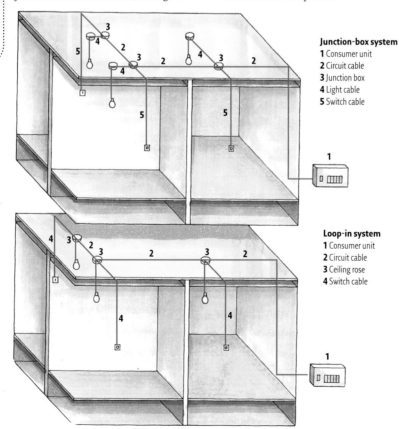

Junction-box system
1 Consumer unit
2 Circuit cable
3 Junction box
4 Light cable
5 Switch cable

Loop-in system
1 Consumer unit
2 Circuit cable
3 Ceiling rose
4 Switch cable

SEE ALSO > Domestic circuits 25, Light fittings 50–1

Identifying connections

When you unscrew a ceiling rose, you can identify what sort of system has been used to wire it by examining the connections closely.

Loop-in system

A loop-in ceiling rose (**1**) has three terminal blocks, arranged in a row. The live (red or brown) wires from the two cut ends of the circuit-feed cable run to the central live block, and the neutral (black or blue) wires run to the neutral block on one side. The earth wires (green-and-yellow) run to a common earth terminal.

The live (red or brown) wire from the switch cable is connected to the remaining terminal in the central live block. The electricity runs through this wire to the switch, then back to the rose via the black 'switch-return' wire, which is connected to the third terminal block (the 'switch-wire block') in the ceiling rose. When the light is 'on', the switch-return wire is live – it is therefore identified by wrapping a piece of red or brown tape round it to distinguish it from the other black or blue wires, which are neutral. The earth wire in the switch cable goes to the common earth terminal.

The brown wire from the pendant flex connects to a terminal in the switch block, while the blue wire runs to the neutral block. If three-core flex is used, the green-and-yellow wire runs to the earth terminal.

When the circuit-feed cable terminates at the last ceiling rose on the circuit, only one set of cable conductors is connected (**2**).

● **Old colour coding**
In a house built before 2005 you are likely to find that the existing cables are colour-coded black for neutral and red for live. The diagrams opposite show old-style lighting-circuit cables. For new-style circuits, substitute brown for red and substitute blue for black.

Junction-box system

The junction boxes on a lighting circuit have four terminals – for live, neutral, earth and switch connections. The live, neutral and earth wires from the circuit cable go to their respective terminals (**3**).

The live (red or brown) wire from the cable that runs to the rose is connected to the switch terminal; the black or blue wire to the neutral terminal; and the green-and-yellow wire to the earth terminal (**3**).

The red or brown wire from the switch cable is connected to the live terminal; the earth wire to the earth terminal; and the black or blue 'return' wire from the switch goes to the switch terminal (**3**). This last conductor must be identified with a piece of red or brown tape wrapped round it.

At the ceiling rose, the live cable wire is connected to one of the outer terminal blocks, and the neutral wire to the other one. The central block is left empty. The earth wire goes to the earth terminal (**4**).

The brown flex wire is connected to the same terminal block as the live cable wire; and the blue flex wire goes to the block holding the neutral cable wire. If the flex has an earth wire, it should be connected to the common earth terminal (**4**).

Replacing a ceiling rose

Turn off the power and remove the circuit fuse or lock off the MCB. Switching off at the wall is not enough. Unscrew the rose cover and examine the connections. If it's a loop-in rose, identify the switch-return wire with red or brown tape. If there's only one live and one neutral wire, it's a junction-box system and there will be no switch cable.

If there are wires running into three terminal blocks, first look for the one with all red or brown wires and no flex wires. This is the live block, containing live circuit-feed wires and a live switch wire. The neutral terminal block takes the black or blue circuit-feed wires and the blue flex wire. The third block takes the brown flex wire plus a black or blue switch-return wire. All earth wires will run to one terminal.

Fixing the new rose
Draw a diagram of the connections before you disconnect the wires. Take down the old backplate. Knock out the entry hole in the new backplate and thread the cables through it; then fix the backplate to the ceiling. If the old fixings aren't secure, screw a piece of wood between the joists above the ceiling (**1**) and drill a hole through it from below for cable access. Screw the new rose backplate to the wood through the ceiling (**2**), and then reconnect the wires.

Slip the new cover over the pendant flex and connect the flex wires to the terminals in the rose – loop these wires over the rose's support hooks to take the weight off the terminals (**3**). Screw on the cover, then switch on the power and test the new light.

1 Screw a platform between the joists

2 Screw the new backplate to the ceiling

3 Loop the flex wires over the support hooks

SEE ALSO > Colour coding 9, Replacing a pendant lampholder 19, Switching off 20

Light fittings

There is a vast range of light fittings for the home – but, although they may differ greatly in their appearance, they can be grouped roughly into eight categories according to their functions.

Close-mounted light

Recessed fitting

Directional recessed light

Wall light

Pendant lights
The pendant light is probably the most common fitting. At its most basic it consists of a lampholder, with a bulb and usually with some kind of shade, and is suspended from a ceiling rose by a length of flexible cord.

Many decorative pendant lights are designed to take more than one bulb and are much heavier than the simpler ones. Heavy pendant lights should never be attached to a standard plastic ceiling rose. However, they can be connected to a detachable ceiling rose.

Close-mounted ceiling lights
A close-mounted fitting is screwed directly to the ceiling, without a ceiling rose, most often by means of a backplate that houses the lampholder or holders. The fitting is usually enclosed by some kind of rigid light-diffuser, which is also attached to the backplate.

Recessed ceiling lights
The lamp housing itself is recessed into the ceiling void, and the diffuser either lies flush with the ceiling or projects only slightly below it. These discreet light fittings, which are ideal for modern interiors with low ceilings, are often referred to as downlighters.

Wall lights
Light fittings designed for screwing to a wall can be supplied either from the lighting circuit in the ceiling void or from a fused spur off a ring circuit. Among the most popular wall lights are uplighters, adjustable spotlights and various kinds of close-mounted fittings.

Batten holders
These basic fittings are fixed directly to the wall or ceiling. They are generally used in areas such as lofts or cellars where appearance is not important.

Batten holder

Track lights
Several individual light fittings can be attached to a metal track screwed to the ceiling or to a wall. Because a contact runs the length of the track, lights can be fitted anywhere along it.

Striplights
These slim lights are often mounted above mirrors and inside cupboards and display cabinets. They can be controlled by separate microswitches so the light comes on each time the cupboard door is opened. Striplights usually take 30W or 60W tubular tungsten-filament lamps with a metal cap at each end.

Some undercupboard striplights are designed to be linked with short lengths of cable so that they can all be powered from a single 13amp plug.

Display alcoves illuminated with striplights

Fluorescent light fittings
A fluorescent light features a glass tube containing mercury vapour. The voltage makes electrons flow between the electrodes at the ends of the tube and bombard an internal coating – which fluoresces, producing bright light.

Different types of coating make the light appear 'warmer' or 'cooler'. For domestic purposes, choose either 'warm white' or 'daylight' tubes.

Fluorescent lighting is unattractive in most domestic interiors, but it is very functional for workshops and garages, where good even illumination is an advantage. However, you should be aware that fluorescent lighting can create the illusion that moving parts of machinery (saw blades and lathe chucks) are stationary when they are still turning.

Light bulbs and tubes

There are numerous light bulbs and tubes designed for use in the various fittings described left.

General lighting service lamps (GLS)
This is the trade name for what we call a light bulb. It is technically known as a tungsten-filament lamp, as the thin metal filament inside the glass envelope glows brightly when heated by electricity.

GLS bulbs come with either an Edison screw or a bayonet fitting for securing the bulb to a lampholder.

The glass envelope can be clear, for fitting inside or behind a glass or plastic cover; or 'pearl', which provides a diffused light for pendant fittings and table lamps. There are also coloured GLS lamps, used mainly for outdoor decoration.

As well as the familiar domed and compact mushroom-shaped bulbs, there are decorative GLS lamps, including bulbs shaped to resemble candle flames.

Reflectors
Some tungsten-filament lamps are silvered to reflect the light forwards or backwards.

Halogen lamps
The filament inside a bulb containing halogen gas glows with an intense white light. As well as mains-voltage lamps, there are low-voltage fittings that have to be wired to a transformer – (see LOW-VOLTAGE LIGHTING).

Fluorescent tubes
Fluorescent tubes are more economical than GLS or halogen bulbs. Compact fluorescent lamps are designed as low-energy replacements for GLS bulbs. Though they are relatively expensive to buy, you are likely to recoup the additional cost within 6 to 12 months.

Light-emitting diodes (LEDs)
Formerly used only for indicator lights, LEDs are now often used in groups to create extremely durable light sources.

The chart opposite compares the features and efficiency of various bulbs and tubes.

SEE ALSO ▶ Lighting circuits 25, Close-mounted lights 52, Fitting a downlighter 52, Fitting track lighting 52, Fluorescent lights 53, Adding wall lights 57, Low-voltage lighting 58–9, Mains-voltage halogen lamps 59

Comparing bulbs and tubes

		Common names	Normal range	Life expectancy in hours	Features	Typical lumens per watt	Colour temperature
• Lumens per watt – the higher the figure, the greater the efficiency (more light per unit of electricity). • Colour temperature (in degrees Kelvin) – the higher the figure, the colder (bluer) the light.							
General service lamp		Light bulb	40–150 watts	1000–2000	General-purpose bulbs in a range of shapes and colours.	12–18	2800
Decorative GLS		Candle, globe	25–60 watts	1000–2000	Bulbs designed to be visible.	7–12	2800
Crown-silvered lamp		Mirrored bulb	40–100 watts	1000–2000	Front of the bulb is coated to bounce light back against a reflective surface inside the light fitting.	8	2700
Internal-silvered lamp		Spotlamp	25–100 watts	1000–2000	The bulb is coated internally to reflect the light forward in a concentrated beam.	8–12.5	2800
Parabolic aluminized reflector		PAR	60–120 watts	1000–2000	Conical-shape reflector, often used for floodlighting.	8–13	3050
Architectural tube		Striplight	25–60 watts	1000–2000	Used to illuminate interior of cabinets and mounted above kitchen worktops.	7–12	2700
Fluorescent tube			13–125 watts	6000–7000	Gives bright, even illumination. A variety of warm and cool tones. Economical to run.	35–100	2700 to 6300
Compact fluorescent tube		Low-energy bulb	48–69 watts	6000–7000	Miniature tubes with Edison screw or bayonet fittings. Cheap to run, lasting 10 to 12 times longer than equivalent GLS bulbs.	6–30	2700 to 6300
Mains-voltage halogen lamp			20–50 watts	2000–4000	Less 'sparkle' than low-voltage halogen, but simpler to install. Popular for wall lights and recessed lighting.	12–16	3050
Linear mains-voltage halogen lamp		Double-ended halogen	100–500 watts	2000–4000	Mainly used for uplighters and floodlights. Tends to get very hot.	18–22	3050
Low-voltage halogen lamp			10–50 watts	2000–4000	Widely used for wall lights and recessed ceiling lights. Can be suspended from special plastic-insulated cable.	14–19	2900 to 3000
Light-emitting diode		LED	Up to 10 watts per light fitting	100,000	Often used for decorative fittings. Can be built into CCTV cameras. Does not get hot.	30–35	5500

SEE ALSO > Fluorescents under cupboards 53, Low-voltage lighting 58–9, Security lighting 61–2, CCTV 63–4

Close-mounted lights

N If you undertake work marked with this symbol, you must inform the BCO before starting – see FIRST THINGS FIRST.

Close-mounted light fittings often have a backplate that screws directly to the ceiling, in place of a ceiling rose. To fit one, switch off the power at the consumer unit and take out the circuit fuse or lock off the MCB, then remove the ceiling rose and fix the new backplate to the ceiling.

If only one cable feeds the light, attach its conductors to the terminals of the lampholder and connect the earth wire to the terminal on the backplate.

Since more heat is generated inside an enclosed fitting, slip heat-resistant sleeving over the conductors before you attach them to their terminals.

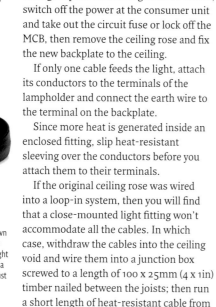

1 BESA boxes
Use a BESA box (also known as a conduit box) to house the connections when a light fitting is supplied without a backplate. A metal box must be earthed.

If the original ceiling rose was wired into a loop-in system, then you will find that a close-mounted light fitting won't accommodate all the cables. In which case, withdraw the cables into the ceiling void and wire them into a junction box screwed to a length of 100 x 25mm (4 x 1in) timber nailed between the joists; then run a short length of heat-resistant cable from the junction box to the new light fitting.

Fittings without backplates
Sometimes close-mounted lights are supplied without backplates.

Wiring Regulations stipulate that all unsheathed wires and terminals have to be enclosed in a noncombustible housing – so if you plan to use a fitting without a backplate, you must find a means of complying. The best way is to fit a BESA box (1), a plastic or metal box that is fixed into the ceiling void so as to lie flush with the ceiling.

The screw-fixing lugs on the BESA box should line up with the fixing holes in the light fitting's coverplate, so check that they do so before buying the box. You will also need two machine screws of the appropriate thread for attaching the light to the box.

Accommodating a BESA box
Check that there isn't a joist directly above where you wish to fit the light (if there is one, move the light to one side until it fits between two joists). Then hold the box against the ceiling, trace round it, and carefully cut the traced shape out of the ceiling with a padsaw.

Cut a platform from timber 25mm (1in) thick to fit between the joists (2), and place it directly over the hole in the ceiling while an assistant marks out the position of the hole on the board from below. Then drill a cable-feed hole centrally through the shape of the ceiling aperture marked on the board. If there's a boss on the back of the BESA box, the hole must be able to accommodate it. Position the box and screw it securely to the platform.

Have your assistant press some kind of flat panel against the ceiling and over the aperture. Fit the BESA box into the aperture from above, so that it rests on the panel; drop the platform over the BESA box, and mark both ends on both joists. Screw a batten to each joist to support the platform at that level. Fix the platform to the battens and feed the cable through the hole in the centre of the BESA box.

For attaching the cable conductors, the light fitting will probably have a plastic connector, which may have three terminals. Alternatively, there may be a separate terminal for the earth conductor attached to the coverplate. After securing the conductors, fix the coverplate to the BESA box with the machine screws.

If the original ceiling rose was fed by more than one cable, connect them to a junction box in the ceiling void, as described previously.

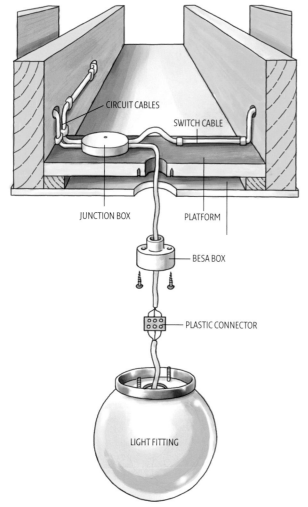

CIRCUIT CABLES

SWITCH CABLE

JUNCTION BOX   PLATFORM

BESA BOX

PLASTIC CONNECTOR

LIGHT FITTING

2 Accommodating a BESA box

Fitting a downlighter

Decide where you want the light, check from above that it falls between joists, and then use the cardboard template supplied with all downlighters to mark the outline of the circular aperture on the ceiling. Drill a series of 12mm (½in) holes just inside the perimeter of the marked circle to remove most of the waste, then cut it out with a padsaw.

Bring a single lighting-circuit cable from a junction box through the sawn opening and attach the cable to the downlighter, following the maker's instructions. You may have to fit another junction box into the void in order to connect the circuit cable to the heat-resistant flex attached to the light fitting.

Insert the downlighter into the opening and secure it there by adjusting the clamps that bear on the hidden upper surface of the ceiling.

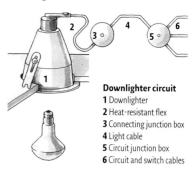

Downlighter circuit
1 Downlighter
2 Heat-resistant flex
3 Connecting junction box
4 Light cable
5 Circuit junction box
6 Circuit and switch cables

Fitting track lighting

Ceiling fixings are supplied with all track-lighting systems. Mount the track so that the terminal-block housing at one end is situated close to where the old ceiling rose was fitted. Pass the circuit cable into the fitting and wire it to the cable connector provided. If the circuit is a loop-in system, mount a junction box in the ceiling void to connect the cables.

Make sure that the number of lights you intend to use on the track will not overload the lighting circuit – which can supply a maximum of eleven 100W lamps (bulbs) or their equivalent.

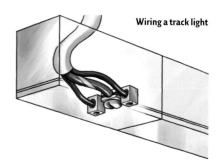

Wiring a track light

SEE ALSO > Building Regulations 8, Switching off 20, Loop-in system 48, Fixing to ceiling 49, Junction box 49, Close-mounted lights 50, Recessed lights 50, Track lights 50

Fluorescent lights

Remove the ceiling rose and then screw the new fluorescent light fitting to the ceiling, positioned so that the circuit cable can be fed into it conveniently.

Fluorescent light fittings are supplied with terminal blocks for connection to the mains supply. Each terminal block will take only three conductors – so either the fitting must be connected to a junction-box system or a junction box must be installed in the ceiling void to accommodate loop-in wiring, as for a close-mounted light (see opposite). Fluorescent lights normally need earth connections, so they can't be used with old systems that lack earth conductors.

You can mount a fluorescent unit by screwing directly into the ceiling joists or into boards nailed between the joists to provide secure fixings.

Replacing a starter

A fluorescent tube needs high voltage in order to start up, and then the voltage is reduced by a ballast unit. Some modern light fittings incorporate an electronic ballast to provide instant or rapid start-up. However, many models still have replaceable electromechanical starters. If the tube merely glows at each end when you switch on, try pressing in and unscrewing the small cylindrical starter, which is usually easily accessible. If that causes the tube to illuminate, buy a new compatible starter for the fitting.

Similarly, a flickering tube may indicate a faulty starter, but it may also mean the tube itself needs replacing. Perform the same test described above.

Replace a faulty starter

Fluorescents under cupboards

You can fit fluorescent lighting underneath wall-mounted kitchen cupboards to illuminate the work surface below. The power is supplied from a switched fused connection unit with a 3amp cartridge fuse.

When installing a second fluorescent light fitting, you can supply it with power by wiring it into the terminal block of the first fitting.

Light switches

The type of switch that's most commonly used for lighting is the plate switch. This has a switch mechanism mounted behind a square faceplate with either one, two or three rockers. Although that's usually enough for domestic purposes, double faceplates with as many as four or six rockers are also available.

A one-way switch simply turns a light on and off. Two-way switches are wired in pairs so that the light can be controlled from two places – typically at the head and foot of a staircase. It's also possible to have an intermediate switch, to allow a light to be controlled from three places.

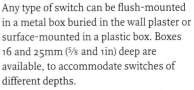

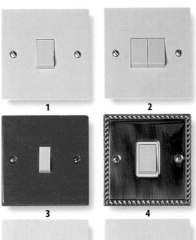

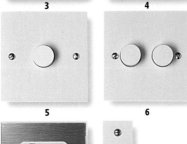

Selection of light switches

1 One-gang rocker switch

2 Two-gang rocker switch

3 Primary-coloured rocker switch

4 Reproduction antique switch

5 One-gang dimmer switch

6 Two-gang dimmer switch

7 Touch dimmer switch

8 Two-gang architrave switch

9 Ceiling switch

Any type of switch can be flush-mounted in a metal box buried in the wall plaster or surface-mounted in a plastic box. Boxes 16 and 25mm (5⁄8 and 1in) deep are available, to accommodate switches of different depths.

Where there is not enough room for a standard switch, a narrow architrave switch can be used. There are double versions with two rockers, one above the other.

As well as turning the light on and off, a dimmer switch controls the intensity of illumination. Some types have a single knob that serves as both switch and dimmer. Others incorporate a separate knob for switching, so the light level does not have to be adjusted every time the light is switched on. Some can be operated by remote control.

The Wiring Regulations forbid the positioning of a conventional switch within reach of a washbasin, bath or shower unit – so only ceiling-mounted double-pole switches with pull-cords must be used in bathrooms. With this type of switch, both live and neutral contacts are broken when it is off.

Installing light switches and cable

Light switches need to be installed in relatively accessible positions, which normally means just inside the door of a room, at about adult shoulder height.

In order to reach the switch, lighting cable is either run within hollow cavity walls or buried in the wall plaster.

Methods for fixing mounting boxes in place are similar to those described for fitting socket outlets.

Choosing switches

Most light switches are made from white plastic, but you can buy other finishes to compliment your decorative scheme. Coloured switches can look striking in a modern house, while reproductions of antique brass switches are both appropriate and attractive in a traditional interior.

SEE ALSO > Building Regulations 8, Fluorescent tubes 50, Replacing switches 54, Adding new switches 55, Two-and-three-way lighting 56

Replacing switches

Replacing a damaged switch is simply a matter of connecting the existing wiring to the terminals of the new switch – making sure that you connect the wires in exactly the same way as in the old one.

● **Switching off**
Always turn off the power and remove the relevant fuse or remove (or lock off) the MCB before you take off a switch faceplate to inspect the wiring.

● **Old colour coding**
In a house built before 2005 you are likely to find the existing cables are colour-coded black for neutral and red for live. The diagrams on this page show old-style switch cables. For new-style circuits, substitute brown for red and substitute blue for black.

(N) If you undertake work marked with this symbol, you must inform the BCO before starting – see FIRST THINGS FIRST.

Check that a new faceplate for a surface-mounted switch will fit the existing mounting box; otherwise, you will have to replace both parts of the switch. If you are able to use the box, attach the new faceplate with the old machine screws. You can then be certain of having screws that will match the threads.

Replacing a one-way switch

Examine a one-way switch and you will see that it is serviced by a two-core-and-earth cable. The earth conductor, if there is one, will be connected to an earth terminal on the mounting box. The red (brown) and black (blue) conductors will be connected to the switch itself.

A true one-way switch has only two terminals, one situated above the other, and the red (brown) or black (blue) conductors can be connected to either terminal (**1**). The back of the faceplate is marked 'top' to ensure that you mount the switch the right way up, so the rocker is depressed when the light is on. The switch

Replacing a two-way switch

A two-way switch will have at least one conductor in each of its three terminals. Without going into the complexities of two-way wiring at this stage, you will find that the most straightforward method of replacing a damaged two-way switch is simply to make a written note of which

Two-gang switches

A two-gang switch is the name for two individual switches mounted on a single faceplate. Each of the switches may be wired differently. One may be working as a one-way switch, and the other as a two-

If you want to replace a surface-mounted switch with a flush-mounted one, remove the old switch then hold the metal box over the position of the original switch and trace round it. Cut away the plaster to the depth of the box, then screw it to the brickwork. Take great care not to damage the existing wiring while you are working.

would work just as well upside down – but the 'up for off' convention is a useful one, as it tells you whether the switch is on or off even when the bulb has failed.

You may come across a light switch that is fed by a two-core-and-earth cable and operates as a one-way switch yet has three terminals (**2**). This is a two-way switch that has been wired for one-way function – something that's fairly common and perfectly safe. If the switch is mounted the right way up, then the red (brown) and black (blue) wires should be connected to the 'Common' and 'L2' terminals (**2**) – either wire to either terminal.

conductors run to which terminals before you start to disconnect the various wires.

Another simple method is to detach the wires from their terminals one at a time, and connect each one to the corresponding terminal on the new two-way switch before you deal with the next conductor.

way (**3**). To transfer the wires from an old switch to the terminals of a new one, work on one switch at a time and use one of the methods for replacing a two-way switch described above.

Replacing a rocker switch with a dimmer switch

Examine the present switch in order to determine the type of wiring that feeds it, then purchase a dimmer switch that will accommodate the existing wiring. The manufacturers of dimmer switches

provide instructions with them, but the connections are basically the same as for ordinary rocker switches (**4**).

Don't use a dimmer switch to control a fluorescent light.

How switches are wired

It is very easy to replace a damaged switch or to swap one for a different type of switch. The illustrations below show four common methods of wiring switches. If a switch appears to be wired differently, it is probably part of a two-way or three-way lighting system. Replace switches as described left.

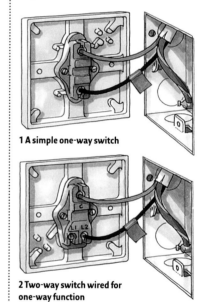

1 A simple one-way switch

2 Two-way switch wired for one-way function

ONE WAY

TWO WAY

3 Two-gang switch for one-way and two-way functions

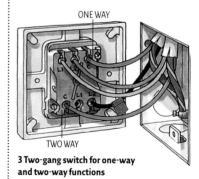

4 Typical dimmer switch

SEE ALSO > Building Regulations 8, Colour coding 9, Switching off 20, Flush mounting 31, Light switches 53, Two-and-three-way lighting 56

Adding new switches and circuits

When you want to move a switch or install a new one, you will have to modify the circuit cables or run a new spur cable from the existing lighting circuit to take the power to where it is needed.

Replacing a wall switch with a ceiling switch

In a bathroom, light switches must be outside zones 0 to 3. If your bathroom has a wall switch that breaks this rule, replace it with a double-pole ceiling switch positioned at least 0.6m (2ft) horizontally from the bath or shower.

Turn off the power at the consumer unit, then remove the old switch. If the cable running up the wall is surface-mounted or in a plastic conduit, pull it up into the ceiling void. It needs to be long enough to reach the point where the new switch will be located.

If the switch cable is buried in the wall, trace it in the ceiling void and cut it. Then wire the remaining part that runs to the light into a three-terminal junction box fixed to a joist or to a piece of wood nailed between two joists. Connect the conductors to separate terminals (1), and from those terminals run a new 1.5mm² two-core-and-earth cable to the site of the ceiling switch.

Bore a hole in the ceiling to pass the cable through to the switch. Screw the switch to a joist if the hole is close enough; otherwise, fix a support board between the joists.

Knock out the entry hole in the back-plate of the switch and pass the cable through, then screw the plate to the ceiling. Strip and prepare the ends of the conductors, connecting the earth wire to the terminal on the backplate. Connect the brown and blue conductors to the terminals on the switch – either wire to either terminal (2). Finally, attach the switch to the backplate and make good any damage done to the plasterwork.

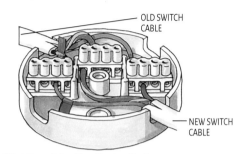

1 Link the switch cable with a junction box

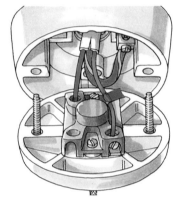

2 Wiring a ceiling switch

• **Old colour coding**
In a house built before 2005 you are likely to find the existing cables are colour-coded black for neutral and red for live. The diagrams on this page show new-style cables being connected to existing old-style circuit cables.

Adding a new switch and light

Switch the power off at the consumer unit and inspect your lighting circuit to check whether it is earthed. If there's no earth wire, get professional advice.

Decide where you want to mount the light, and bore a hole through the ceiling for the cable. If the ceiling rose can't be screwed to a joist, nail a board between two joists to provide a strong fixing for the rose.

Bore another hole right above the site of the new switch and close to the wall. Push twists of paper through both holes, so you can find them easily from above. Screw the switch mounting box to the wall and cut a chase in the plaster for the cable, up to the hole already bored in the ceiling.

Your new light fitting can be supplied with power from a nearby junction box or ceiling rose that's already on the lighting circuit – or, if it's more convenient, from a new junction box wired into the lighting-circuit cable. From whichever of these sources you choose, run a 1.5mm² two-core-and-earth cable to the position of the new light fitting – but don't connect to the lighting circuit till the new installation has been completed. Push the end of the cable through the hole in the ceiling and identify it with tape marked 'Mains'.

The next step is to run a similar cable from the switch to the same lighting point and identify it with tape marked 'Switch'.

Strip and prepare the cable at the switch, connecting the earth wire to the terminal on the mounting box – and connect the brown and blue conductors, either wire to either terminal if it is a one-way switch. If you are using a two-way switch, connect the brown wire to the 'Common' terminal and the blue wire to 'L2'. Screw the switch to the box.

Knock out the cable-entry hole in the ceiling rose and feed both cables through it, then screw the rose to the ceiling.

Take the cable marked 'Mains' and connect its brown conductor to the live central block and its blue one to the neutral block. Slip a green-and-yellow sleeve over the earth wire and connect it to the earth terminal.

Connect the brown wire of the switch cable to the live block, and the blue wire to the switch-wire block: mark the blue wire with brown tape. Connect the switch earth wire to the earth terminal. Connect the pendant flex and screw on the rose cover.

With the power turned off, connect the new light circuit to the old one at the rose or junction box. The new conductors will have to share terminals with the old wires already connected: brown to live, blue to neutral, and earth to earth (see right) Finally, test and switch on the new circuit.

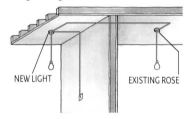

Circuit for a new light
You can take the power for a new light from an existing ceiling rose or junction box, or insert a new junction box into the existing lighting circuit.

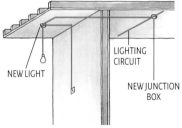

Lighting cable connected to a loop-in rose

SEE ALSO > Building Regulations 8, Bathroom zones 11, Testing circuits 12–13, Switching off 20, Important notes at consumer unit 22, Stripping cable 26, Running cable 27–9, Junction box 33, Lighting circuits 48, Wiring a rose 48–9, Fixing to ceiling 49, Circuit lengths 68

Two-and-three way lighting

There are situations in which a light should be controllable from two points. For example, a landing light needs to be controlled from both the top and bottom of the stairs.

Adding a two-way light

Installing a new two-way light is very similar to installing a one-way light, the only real difference being in the wiring of the switches.

First, mount the ceiling rose and both of the two-way switches, then run a 1.5mm² two-core-and-earth cable from the power source to the light and from the light to the nearest switch. Don't connect the new installation to the lighting circuit until all the wiring has been completed.

Run a 1.5mm² three-core-and-earth cable from the first to the second switch. Then strip the conductors and prepare them for connecting to the switches, slipping insulating sleeves over the bare earth wires.

At the first switch you will have two cables to connect: the switch cable from the light and the one linking the two switches. The switch cable has three conductors (brown, blue and green-and-yellow); the

linking cable has four (brown, black, grey and green-and-yellow). Connect the green-and-yellow wires from both cables to the earth terminal on the mounting box (**1**). Next, connect the brown wire from the linking cable to the 'Common' terminal on the switch. Connect the black wire and either the brown or blue switch-cable wire to the 'L1' terminal. Connect the grey wire and the remaining switch-cable wire to 'L2' (**1**). Screw the switch's faceplate to the mounting box.

At the second switch, connect the linking cable's green-and-yellow wire to the earth terminal; its brown wire to the 'Common' terminal; its black wire to 'L1'; and its grey wire to 'L2' (**1**). Screw the switch's faceplate to the box.

Make sure the power is switched off, and then connect the installation to the lighting circuit at either a ceiling rose or a junction box. Finally, test the new installation.

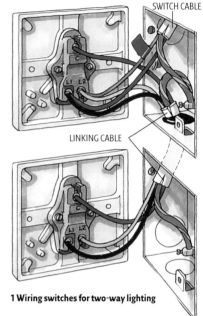

1 Wiring switches for two-way lighting

Three-way lighting

You can control a light from three places by adding an intermediate switch to the circuit described above. The intermediate switch interrupts the three-core-and-earth cable linking the other two. It has two 'L1' and two 'L2' terminals.

At its mounting box you will have two identical sets of wires – brown, black, grey and green-and-yellow. Connect the green-

and-yellow wires to the earth terminal on the box (**2**) and join the two brown wires – which play no part in the intermediate switching – with a plastic connector (**2**).

Connect the grey and black wires of either cable to the 'L1' terminals on the new switch and those of the other cable to the 'L2' terminals (**2**). Then screw the faceplate to the mounting box.

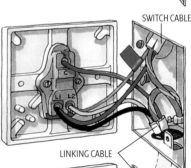

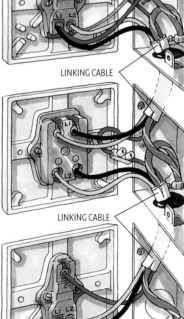

2 Wiring switches for three-way lighting

Two-way lighting
(right)
1 Consumer unit
2 Light fitting
3 Lighting-circuit cable
4 Switch cable
5 Switch
6 Linking cable
7 Junction box

Three-way lighting
(far right)
1 Consumer unit
2 Light fitting
3 Lighting-circuit cable
4 Switch cable
5 Switch
6 Intermediate switch
7 Linking cable
8 Junction box

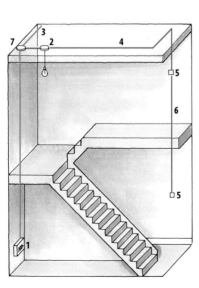

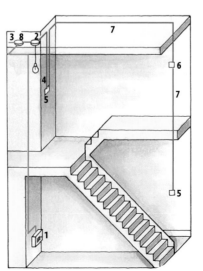

SEE ALSO > Testing circuits 12–13, Switching off 20, Cable 26, Running cable 27–9, Connecting to junction boxes 33, Lighting circuits 48, Adding new switch and light 55, Connecting to loop-in rose 55, Circuit lengths 68

Adding wall lights

Many wall lights are supplied without integral backplates to enclose the wires and connections. To comply with the Wiring Regulations, such a fitting must be attached to a noncombustible mounting such as a BESA box – a round plastic or metal box that's screwed to the wall in a recess chopped out of the plaster and brickwork.

Alternatively, you can use an architrave-switch mounting box. This is a slim box that will leave plenty of room on each side for the wallplug fixings needed for the light fitting. Both types of mounting box are fixed to the wall in the same way as the boxes used for flush-mounted socket outlets.

The basic circuit and connections

The simplest way to connect wall lights to the lighting circuit is via a junction box. The procedure is to complete the wall-light installation first, then switch off the electricity and connect the new installation to the junction box.

Wire up a one-way switch. All the wall lights in the room will be controlled by this switch – although lights with integral switches can be controlled individually, too.

Next, run a 1.5mm² two-core-and-earth cable from the junction box, looping in and out of each wall-light mounting to the last one, where the cable ends.

Prepare the cut ends of the conductors for connection. At each of the lights, slip green-and-yellow sleeving over the earth wires and connect them to the earth terminal on the mounting box.

Connect up the brown and blue wires to the block connector inside each light fitting – connecting the blue conductors to the terminal already holding the blue wire, and the brown conductors to the terminal already holding the brown wire.

The last wall-light mounting will have one end of the cable entering it; connect the wires as described above.

Using an architrave-switch mounting box

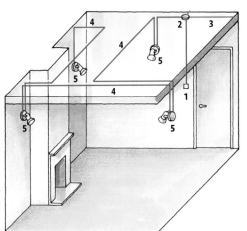

Basic wall-light circuit
The basic circuit and connections are as described above.
1 Switch
2 Junction box
3 Existing lighting circuit
4 1.5mm² wall-light cable
5 Wall light

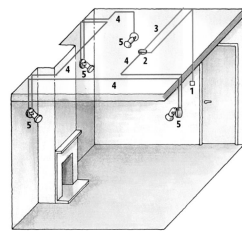

Replacing a ceiling light
You can dispense with a ceiling light in favour of wall lights, using the existing wiring and switch. Switch off the power, then remove the rose and connect up the wiring to a fixed junction box.
1 Existing switch and cable
2 Junction box replaces rose
3 Existing lighting circuit
4 1.5mm² wall-light cable
5 Wall light

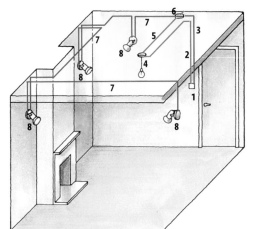

Ceiling light plus wall lights
If you want to retain your ceiling light, you can substitute a two-gang switch for the single one – and wire the present ceiling-light cable to one half of the switch, and the new wall-lighting cable to the other half.
1 Two-gang switch
2 Old switch cable
3 New switch cable
4 Ceiling light
5 Existing lighting circuit
6 Junction box
7 1.5mm² wall-light cable
8 Wall light

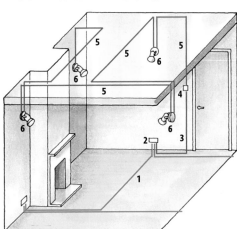

Using a spur
Wall lights can be wired to a ring circuit by means of a spur cable. Run a 2.5mm² two-core-and-earth spur from a nearby socket to a switched fused connection unit that has a 3amp fuse.
1 Ring circuit
2 Socket outlet
3 Spur cable
4 Fused connection unit
5 1.5mm² wall-light cable
6 Wall light

SEE ALSO > Testing circuits 12–13, Switching off 20, Cable 26, Running cable 27–9, Running a spur 33, Fused connection units 34, Lighting circuits 48, Light fittings 50, Light switches 53, Circuit lengths 68

Low-voltage lighting

Originally, low-voltage halogen light fittings were developed for illuminating commercial premises. Being small and unobtrusive, they blend into any scheme and the bright intense beams of light they produce are ideal for display lighting. The potential for dramatic effects and narrowly focused task lighting was not lost on home owners, and manufacturers were quick to respond with a range of low-voltage fittings.

N If you undertake work marked with this symbol, you must inform the BCO before starting – see FIRST THINGS FIRST.

The specially designed miniature bulb is the key to what makes low-voltage lighting so attractive. The light source is concentrated into a small filament, which enables accurate focusing of spotlight beams. The integral 'dichroic' reflector allows the heat generated by the filament to escape backward into the fitting, creating a cool but intense white light. Coloured bulbs are also available for special effects and mood lighting.

Low-voltage light fittings

Miniature fixed or adjustable 'eyeball' downlighters recessed into the ceiling are among the most widely used low-voltage light fittings. They can be mounted individually or wired in groups to a transformer, which is also concealed in the space above the ceiling. Some fittings are made with integral transformers; these include table lamps and small spotlights. Others, such as track lights, combine several individual fittings connected to a single transformer. Unique to low-voltage lighting are fittings connected to exposed plastic-sheathed cables suspended across the room.

Low-voltage halogen bulb

Optimum voltage

Even a small increase from the designed voltage can halve the life of a bulb. If the voltage is too low, light output drops and eventually the bulb blackens. Voltage can be affected in a number of ways, and you need to select your equipment accordingly.

Choose a transformer with an output that closely matches the combined wattage of the bulbs on the circuit. It's important to ensure that the total wattage of these bulbs is greater than 70 per cent of the transformer rating, or the bulbs will burn out relatively quickly. For example, a 50W transformer can supply two 20W bulbs or one 50W. A 200W transformer is perfect for four 50W bulbs, but not for six 20W bulbs (for these, you would want a 150W transformer). If you buy a low-voltage kit, you can be sure the transformer is suitable. Even with a perfectly matched transformer, replace a blown bulb as soon as possible to avoid overloading the other bulbs on the circuit.

Dimmer switches

Using ordinary dimmer switches is not advisable, because they too reduce voltage to an unacceptable level. For this type of control, check that the low-voltage fittings are suitable for dimming and only use dimmer switches specifically designed for low-voltage lighting.

Using separate components **N**

If you install a low-voltage lighting kit that comes ready-wired (see opposite), there is no need to notify your Building Control Officer except when it is fitted in a special location such as a kitchen or bathroom. However, if for some reason it is not convenient to use this type of kit, it is possible to install low-voltage lighting, using individual components, such as light fittings, transformer and cable. However this type of work is notifiable.

Having decided on the ideal location of each light fitting, choose a central position for the transformer.

The connections of the mains-voltage supply and switching would be the same as the kit system shown opposite. However, on the low-voltage side, use a separate 1.5mm² two-core cable for each light fitting, keeping this as short as possible – a maximum of 4 metres from each fitting to the output terminals of the transformer. Normally, each light fitting is supplied with a terminal block for connecting its heat-resistant flex to the cable.

If necessary, you can install longer cables to each light fitting, but this would involve calculating the larger cable sizes required.

Low-voltage fittings
These light fittings take their power from special plastic-coated low-voltage cable that stretches from wall to wall. This system is unique to low-voltage lighting.

SEE ALSO > Building Regulations 8, Cables 26, Dimmer switches 53

Installing a ready-wired lighting kit

There is no need to notify your Building Control Officer if you install a ready-wired low-voltage kit, provided it is CE marked and it is not in a special location, such as a bathroom or kitchen. The circuit described here includes a kit with a transformer, supplying three individual halogen lamps of equal wattage.

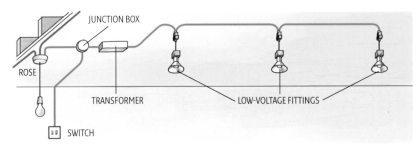

JUNCTION BOX

ROSE

TRANSFORMER   LOW-VOLTAGE FITTINGS

SWITCH

Making the connections

Place the transformer at a convenient point for the light fittings – the maximum spacing of these fittings is limited by the length of the flex supplied. Screw the transformer to a joist, between the ceiling and the floorboards above. Clear any insulation from around the transformer.

Screw a four-terminal junction box to the joist close to the transformer. Prepare the flex already connected to the input side of the transformer and connect this to the switch-wire and neutral terminals in the junction box. From the same box, run a 1.5mm² two-core-and-earth cable to the switch position, and a circuit-feed cable of similar size to the nearest ceiling rose, where you will pick up the 230V mains supply (but don't make this connection yet). Make all the connections at the junction box as shown (**1**).

Each light fitting has a special plug attached to the back of the lamp by a short length of heat-resistant flex. Insert this plug into the matching socket on the flex supplied with the kit (**2**) – then clip this flex to a joist to make sure it cannot touch the back of any of the light fittings, which can become hot. Keep this low-voltage flex separate from any cable carrying mains-voltage electricity. At the transformer, connect the flex to the output terminals (**3**) as described in the manufacturer's instructions.

Fit an ordinary wall switch to control the lighting (**4**).

Connecting to the mains

Having turned off the power, connect the live, neutral and earth wires of the circuit-feed cable to the ceiling rose (**5**).

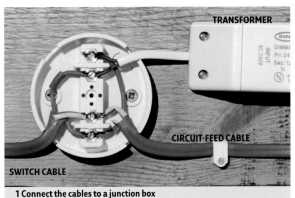

TRANSFORMER

CIRCUIT-FEED CABLE

SWITCH CABLE

1 Connect the cables to a junction box

Take power from the nearest ceiling rose

2 Connect the cable to the light fitting

3 Connect live and neutral wires to output terminals

4 Wire the wall switch

NEW CIRCUIT-FEED CABLE

5 Switch off and connect cable to the ceiling rose

Mains-voltage halogen

You can buy mains-voltage halogen fittings that are very similar in appearance to the low-voltage versions. Their main advantage is that they don't require a remote transformer to reduce the power to 12V and can therefore be connected to existing wiring, like other mains-voltage fittings. However, the bulbs and fittings are generally more expensive than the low-voltage equivalents.

● **230V halogen**
All extra-low-voltage wiring is notifiable, but wiring 230V fittings is only notifiable in special locations.

With some mains-voltage ranges, an electronic transformer is built into the base of each bulb. As a result, the filament within the bulb operates on 12V, just like any other low-voltage fitting. This type of bulb is usually made with an Edison-screw end cap.

Most ranges of mains-voltage fittings accommodate a bulb with two pins that engage a spring-loaded lampholder, similar in principle to the familiar bayonet-cap bulbs. These bulbs contain quartz burners that operate on 230V.

Mains-voltage fittings emit the same sort of bright, sparkling illumination that is normally associated with low-voltage lighting – but if you want a lamp with a relatively cool output, make sure you choose mains-voltage bulbs made with dichroic reflectors, rather than the aluminium-coated versions.

SEE ALSO > Building Regulations 8, Switching off 20, Cable 26, Running cable 27–9

Using electricity outdoors

Electrical work in the garden is subject to the same regulations that govern wiring inside the house. Indeed, you are required to notify the BCO before you install any exterior electrical fittings, except for ready-wired plug-in kits and solar powered lights and pumps.

Despite these restrictions, there are good reasons for extending your electrical installation outside the house. First, and most important, it is safer to run electric garden tools from a convenient, properly protected socket than to trail long leads from unsuitable sockets inside the house – a practice that can lead to serious accidents. A garage or workshop is also safer and more efficient if it is equipped with good lighting and its own circuit from which to run power tools.

Finally, well-arranged lighting and waterfalls or fountains powered by electric pumps add to the charm of a garden or patio and can extend its use in summer by providing a pleasing background for barbecues and outdoor parties.

N If you undertake work marked with this symbol, you must inform the BCO before starting – see FIRST THINGS FIRST.

Socket with integral RCD

Adaptor RCDs plug into any socket outlet

Installing a socket for garden tools **N**

The Wiring Regulations stipulate that any socket outlet supplying mains power to garden tools or equipment has to be protected by a residual current device (RCD) with a trip rating of 30 milliamps. This applies to any socket, including one indoors which could reasonably be used to power an outside appliance. The RCD will switch off the power as soon as it detects a fault, long before anyone using the equipment can receive a fatal electric shock.

Outdoors or indoors?
There are special external waterproof socket outlets. These are best installed by a qualified electrician able to satisfy the requirements of the BCO.

You can use an ordinary socket, provided it is protected by an RCD and is housed in a weatherproof workshop, garage, lobby or conservatory that's part of the house. Mount this type of socket high enough to prevent it being struck by a wheelbarrow or hidden by garden tools.

Providing RCD protection
You can provide RCD protection in several ways. Perhaps the best method is to have a consumer unit with its own built-in RCD, or to fit a separate RCD near the consumer unit so that it protects the whole ring circuit, including any spurs for garden equipment. Alternatively, install a socket that incorporates an RCD.

RCDs fitted in plug-in adaptors will provide some protection, but they do not satisfy the requirement for the socket itself to be protected.

Fitting a porch light **N**

A light illuminating the entrance welcomes visitors to your home and helps them to identify the house. It also enables you to view unexpected callers before you open the door. Choose a light that is specifically designed for outdoor use – the fitting must be weatherproof, and the bulb has to be held in a moisture-proof rubber gasket or cup that surrounds the electrical connections.

If possible, position the porch light in such a way that the cable to it can be run straight through the wall or ceiling of the porch, directly into the back of the fitting. But if an ordinary cable has to be run along an outside wall, it must be protected by being passed through a length of plastic conduit.

A porch light can be installed by a procedure very similar to that for adding a new light indoors. Take the power from the nearest ceiling rose – probably in the entrance hall – and run it to a 5amp four-terminal junction box screwed to a board between ceiling joists. From the junction box, run a 1.5mm² two-core-and-earth cable to a switch mounted near the door and run a similar cable to the light fitting itself.

Bore a hole through the wall where you plan to position the light. Cement a short length of plastic conduit into the hole, using a soft rubber grommet to seal each end of the tube.

Run the cable through the conduit and wire it to the fitting, following the manufacturer's instructions. With the power switched off, connect the porch-light cable at the ceiling rose.

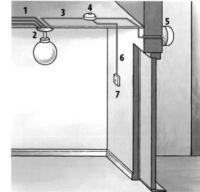

Porch-light circuit
1 Loop-in circuit and switch cables
2 Ceiling rose
3 1.5mm² lighting cable
4 Junction box
5 Porch light
6 Switch cable
7 Porch-light switch

SEE ALSO > Building Regulations 8, Testing circuits 12–13, Switching off 20, RCDs 21, 22, Running cable 27–9, Running a spur 33, Lighting circuits 48, Junction box 48, One-way switch 54, Adding a new light 55, Connecting to a loop-in rose 55, Circuit lengths 68

Security lighting

Any form of exterior lighting that illuminates the approaches to your house and garage allows you to move about your home with greater convenience and safety – and if it's controlled automatically, it saves you having to fumble with your door keys in the dark. However, probably higher on most people's list of priorities is the added security afforded by installing a system that will detect the presence of intruders and draw attention to their activities.

Dusk-to-dawn lighting

You cannot feel completely secure if you have to remember to switch on exterior lighting every evening. The simplest solution is to install exterior light fittings that are controlled automatically by the ambient light level. Known as dusk-to-dawn lights, these fittings create permanently illuminated areas during the hours of darkness. A photocell detects a change in the level of daylight, switching the lamp on at the approach of darkness and off again early in the morning. For larger properties, install a single photocell that controls a number of ordinary exterior light fittings.

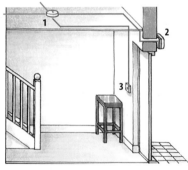

Wiring dusk-to-dawn security lighting
1 Junction box inserted in existing lighting circuit.
2 Light fitting with built-in photocell.
3 Wall switch.

The circuit

From a junction box installed in your domestic lighting circuit, run a 1.5mm² two-core-and-earth cable to the light fitting and another cable of the same size from the junction box to an ordinary wall switch. If you want to install more than one light fitting, run the cable from the junction box to each light in turn, using the single switch to control all of them.

Adjusting security lighting

A screw is usually provided for adjusting the sensitivity of the photocell. Wait till it is getting dark; then turn on the wall switch and gradually adjust the screw until the light comes on. The photocell will operate the lighting, provided the wall switch is left on.

Installing a light fitting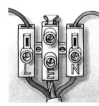

Plan the installation carefully, making sure the light fitting is mounted high enough to prevent unauthorized interference. Drill a cable-access hole through the wall, and line it with a short length of plastic conduit (see FITTING A PORCH LIGHT, opposite). Pass a length of cable through the hole in the wall and into the back of the fitting. Screw the light fitting to the wall.

Inside the fitting, cut the separate conductors to length, leaving enough slack to reach their separate terminals. Connect the blue conductor to the neutral terminal and the brown one to the live terminal – these may have internal wiring already connected to them (**1**). Fit green-and-yellow sleeving over the bare earth conductor and connect it to the earth terminal. It may be necessary to connect internal wires to the photocell before the bulb is fitted and the cover replaced.

Now run the cable from the light fitting to where you are going to connect up to the lighting circuit.

Mounting the light switch

Cut the cable chase in the plaster and mount a plastic or metal box on the wall for the switch. Then run the cable into the mounting box, and connect the blue and brown conductors to the terminals of a simple one-way switch (**2**). Sleeve the earth conductor and connect it to the earth terminal in the mounting box. Screw the faceplate to the mounting box, then take the cable to the point in the lighting circuit where you plan to install the junction box.

1 Wiring the light fitting

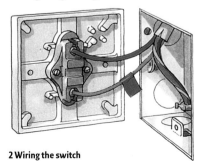

2 Wiring the switch

Connecting to the lighting circuit

The power must be switched off at the consumer unit, and the lighting-circuit fuse removed or the MCB removed or locked off. Cut the lighting cable in order to install a four-terminal junction box. Screw the box securely to a joist. The terminals in the box, which are normally unmarked, should be designated as live, neutral, earth and switch.

Prepare the cut ends of the lighting-circuit cable and connect the live, neutral and earth conductors to their respective terminals (**3**).

Prepare the end of the cable running from the light fitting and connect its brown conductor to the switch terminal (**3**). Connect its blue conductor to the neutral terminal, and its sheathed earth conductor to the earth terminal.

Prepare the end of the cable running from the switch and then connect its brown conductor to the live terminal, the sleeved earth conductor to the earth terminal, and the blue conductor to the switch terminal (**3**). Identify this last conductor by wrapping a piece of brown tape round it. Make sure all the connections are secure, and then refit the cover of the junction box.

If the new circuit tests satisfactorily, the power supply can be switched back on at the consumer unit.

° **Old colour coding**
In a house built before 2005 you are likely to find the existing cables are colour-coded black for neutral and red for live. The diagram below shows new-style cable being connected to existing old-style circuit cable.

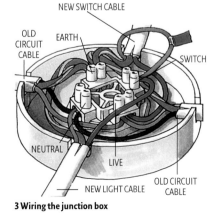

NEW SWITCH CABLE
OLD CIRCUIT CABLE
EARTH
SWITCH
NEUTRAL
LIVE
NEW LIGHT CABLE
OLD CIRCUIT CABLE

3 Wiring the junction box

SEE ALSO > Building Regulations 8, Testing circuits 12–13, Switching off 20, Important notes at consumer unit 22, Running cable 27–9, Lighting circuits 48, Infra-red lighting 62, Circuit lengths 68

Passive infra-red lighting

Exterior lights connected to a passive infra-red detector illuminate only when the sensor picks up the body heat of someone within range. The detector is also fitted with a photocell, so the lights operate only at night.

N If you undertake work marked with this symbol, you must inform the BCO before starting – see FIRST THINGS FIRST.

A passive infra-red system has two advantages over simple dusk-to-dawn lighting. A porch light, for example, switches on only as you or visitors approach the entrance, then switches off again after a set period. This means you're not wasting electricity by burning a lamp continuously all night. Secondly, remote passive infra-red detectors can be positioned to detect an intruder almost anywhere around your home and will switch on all your security lights or only those you think necessary. The effect is likely to startle intruders and deter them from approaching any further.

Light fittings and sensors

Because infra-red detectors are designed to be mounted about 2.5m (8ft) above ground level, light fittings made with integral detectors tend to be for porch lighting and most of them are styled accordingly. However, since the lighting needs to be operated for periods of no more than a few minutes at a time, remote infra-red detectors are often used to control powerful halogen floodlights. Floodlights are also available with built-in detectors, which simplifies the wiring.

Security lighting
1 Remote passive infra-red detector
2 Halogen floodlight
3 Porch light with integral detector

Positioning detectors

Unless you position detectors carefully, your security lighting will be activated unnecessarily. This can be a nuisance to neighbours and, as with any security device that's constantly giving false alarms, you will soon begin to mistrust it and ignore its warnings.

Infra-red detectors have sensitivity controls so that they won't be activated by moving foliage or the presence of small animals. However, if your house is close to a footpath, you will need to adjust the angle of the detectors so that the lights don't switch on every time a pedestrian passes by.

When fitting a remote detector, make sure it isn't aimed directly at a floodlight that it is controlling – or its photocell will try to switch it off as soon as it comes on and the likely result will be a light that simply flickers and never fully illuminates the scene.

It is also important not to position an infra-red detector above a balanced flue from a boiler, or any other source of heat that could activate the sensor.

The circuit

It is usually possible to wire infra-red security lighting in exactly the same way as dusk-to-dawn lighting. However, as some detectors are capable of controlling several powerful floodlights, you may not be able to run them from the domestic lighting circuit. In which case, you will need to run a 2.5mm² two-core-and-earth spur from a power circuit and control the lighting with a switched fused connection unit.

Use a 3amp fuse in the connection unit for a combined rating of up to 690W; a 13amp fuse for anything greater.

Wiring a remote sensor **N**

Unless the manufacturer's instructions suggest an alternative method, wire an individual light fitting with an integral infra-red detector in the same manner as a dusk-to-dawn fitting.

To wire a remote sensor controlling light fittings mounted elsewhere, take the incoming cable from the junction box or fused connection unit into the back of the fitting and connect its brown and blue conductors to the 'Mains' terminals. Run a second cable of the same size from the 'Load' terminals back through the wall and on to the first light fitting. Sleeve both bare copper earth conductors and connect them to the earth terminal.

Wire the first light fitting using the method described for a dusk-to-dawn fitting, then connect another cable to the same terminals and run it on to the second light fitting, and so on.

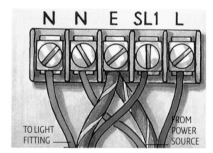

Wiring a remote sensor

Adjusting detectors

Once all the connections are made, you need to set the infra-red detector's adjustment knobs or screws. One of them is for setting the photocell so that the system operates only during the hours of darkness. A second control dictates the period of time that the lights will remain on – three or four minutes should be sufficient.

The final operation is to set the sensor's controls

SEE ALSO > Building Regulations 8, Switching off 20, Running cable 27–9, Running a spur 33, Fused connection units 34, Lighting circuits 48, Dusk-to-dawn lighting 61, Circuit lengths 68

Closed-circuit television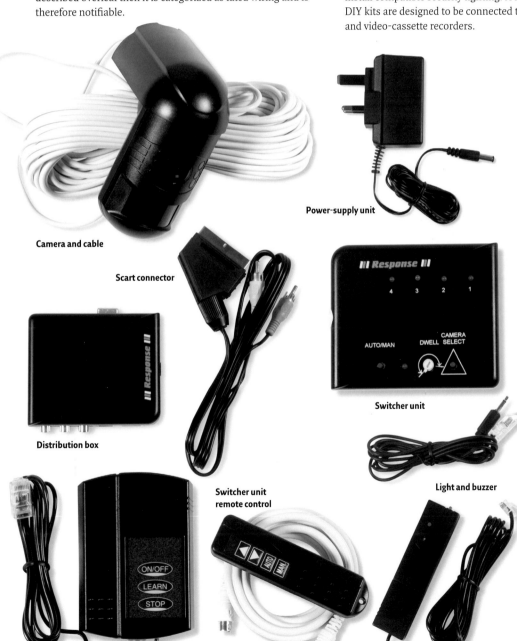

Surveillance by closed-circuit television acts as a deterrent to would-be intruders – and if you choose to record the output from your cameras, in the event of a burglary it may help the police to apprehend the perpetrator and recover your stolen property.

There are numerous CCTV systems at your disposal, including highly sophisticated equipment primarily designed for protecting commercial premises. You are required to notify the BCO before installing most types of CCTV system, but if you choose one of the relatively inexpensive but effective plug-in DIY kits you can install it yourself without notification. However, if a kit is installed as described overleaf then it is categorized as fixed wiring and is therefore notifiable.

Do-it-yourself kits

Not every CCTV kit contains the same equipment, but illustrated below is a selection of accessories sold for DIY installation. Light fittings are rarely, if ever, included in these kits, but since a great many attempted burglaries occur after dark, it's hardly worth the expense of installing CCTV unless you are prepared to buy and install compatible security lighting. A monitor is not required, as DIY kits are designed to be connected to ordinary television sets and video-cassette recorders.

Camera and cable

Power-supply unit

Scart connector

Distribution box

Switcher unit

Switcher unit remote control

Light and buzzer

VCR controller

Extension cable

Cameras
Up to four cameras can be connected to the average CCTV system. Black-and-white cameras are the least expensive and tend to give a sharper image in low light levels. Most cameras incorporate a microphone, and some have built-in PIR (passive infra-red) movement detectors.

Power-supply unit
CCTV power-supply units have built-in 13amp plugs. There are heater elements in the cameras to prevent condensation, so they have to be connected to the electrical supply permanently. Power consumption, however, is negligible.

Distribution box
This compact unit sends the signals from the camera to your television set. You can make the connection using phono plugs, but a Scart connector is preferable.

Switcher unit
You will only need a switcher unit if you have more than one camera. Connected to the distribution box, it has a socket for each camera input.

VCR controller
This device switches on your VCR when a camera detects movement in the vicinity of your house.

Audible warning
A buzzer will alert you when a camera picks up a possible intruder, even when your TV set is switched off. The unit, which also includes a small flashing light, plugs into the distribution box.

Cable
Special colour-coded multi-core cable transmits the signals from the camera to your TV set. It is supplied in standard lengths, and extension cables are available.

SEE ALSO > Building Regulations 8, Security lighting 61–2, Installing CCTV 64

Installing CCTV

Although the type of plug-in kit described below is designed for DIY installation, the installation of such a system becomes notifiable if fixed wiring and external security lighting are used.

Installing a plug-in system

Single camera
The simplest CCTV installation consists of a single camera, a distribution box and a television set.

N If you undertake work marked with this symbol, you must inform the BCO before starting – see FIRST THINGS FIRST.

Try to cover the most likely approaches to your home. Adjust each camera so it is aimed at a slight angle to the route an intruder might take. It will then record him from several different angles as he passes by. This may help the police identify a known burglar.

Place your CCTV cameras out of reach – somewhere between 2.5 and 3m (8 to 10ft) from the ground. Point each camera down at an angle, never directly into the sun or towards a light fitting. If you have PIR detectors fitted to the cameras, make sure they are adjusted to avoid false alarms being triggered by passing animals and moving branches.

If you're in doubt about the suitability of a particular location, it may make sense to rig up a temporary connection and test the camera before you install it.

Running and connecting cable

Run the cable supplied with the kit from the camera to the television set, keeping as much of the wiring indoors as possible. Clip the cable to a sound surface at 1m (3ft) intervals, making sure it does not run alongside mains power cables.

To make it more difficult for anyone to tamper with the connections, feed the cable through a hole drilled directly behind the camera's housing.

It is inadvisable to coil up excess cable. Instead, cut it to length and feed the cut end though the grommet or seal in the camera mounting; then prepare and connect the colour-coded wires to the camera terminal box, following the manufacturer's instructions.

Installing the distribution box

Install the distribution box behind your television set. Plug the Scart connector into the back of the set, and the DIN connector on the camera cable into the distribution box. Connect the power-supply unit to the distribution box and plug it into a convenient 13amp socket.

Security lighting

To use cameras effectively after dark, install porch lighting or, better still, floodlights fitted with PIR detectors. Since some cameras are particularly sensitive to infra-red, it pays to choose fittings that take halogen or tungsten bulbs rather than fluorescents. Try to achieve even illumination – it is difficult for a camera to cope with strong contrasts between, say, a dark carport and a well-lit pathway.

Alternatively, buy the type of camera that can detect an image in the very low level of illumination produced by light-emitting diodes mounted round the lens. No other form of security lighting is required with this type of camera.

Recording intruders

Recording the signals
With a more complex installation, you can have several cameras connected to a VCR or DVR so you can make a recording of would-be intruders.

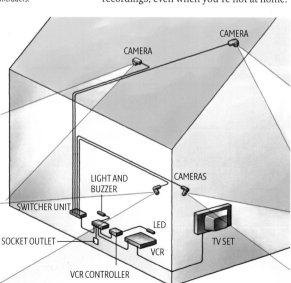

If you want to tape the pictures transmitted from your cameras, plug the Scart connector into a video recorder instead of the TV set. Switch the TV to the video channel, and the VCR to the AUX (auxiliary) channel. This gives you the option to make recordings, even when you're not at home.

Switching channels

Provided that you leave your TV set switched to the video channel, your TV viewing will be interrupted to show you the scene outside as soon as a camera detects an intruder. You will still be able to switch from one TV channel to another, using the standard VCR remote controller.

Recording the scene

If you want the VCR to start recording whenever the camera's PIR detects movement, fit a special VCR controller to the distribution box and point its infra-red output at the port used by your standard VCR remote controller.

If you prefer, you can fit a small unobtrusive LED (light-emitting diode) extension to the controller, so that you can hide the main unit out of sight.

You can preset how long you want the VCR to continue recording before it automatically switches off.

Using a second VCR

With your VCR switched to the AUX channel, you won't be able to view a pre-recorded tape – so you may want to buy a cheap second-hand VCR that you can use solely for surveillance. You could install this VCR somewhere out of sight, so that a burglar is less likely to spot it and destroy the evidence.

Linking to several TV sets

You can use all the television sets in your home as surveillance monitors, but to do this the signals have to be transmitted via the TV aerial. For multi-set monitoring, you need to connect the distribution box to a device known as a modulator. Connect the TV aerial to the modulator, and the modulator to your existing aerial splitter socket.

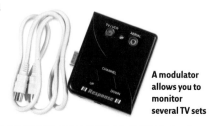

A modulator allows you to monitor several TV sets

Garden lighting and pumps

Just a few outdoor lights can transform a garden. Spotlights or floodlighting can be used to emphasize particularly attractive features, at the same time providing functional lighting for pathways and steps.

Extra-low-voltage lighting

Some types of garden light fitting are connected directly to the mains supply. However, there are also very efficient systems that draw power via an extra-low-voltage transformer. Position the transformer close to a 13amp socket outlet in a garage or workshop, and connect it to the socket by an ordinary square-pin plug. The flex – which is normally supplied with the light fitting – is connected to the two 12V outlet terminals on the transformer.

Carry out the connections to the lights in accordance with the manufacturer's instructions.

Unless the maker states otherwise, extra-low-voltage flex supplying garden lights can be run along the ground without further protection – but inspect it regularly and don't let it trail over stone steps or other sharp edges likely to damage the PVC insulation if someone steps on it. If you have to extend flex, use a purpose-made waterproof connector.

Pool lighting

Pool lights are normally submerged so as to have at least 18mm (¾ in) of water above the lens. Some are designed to float unless they're held down below the surface by smooth stones, carefully placed on the flex.

Submerged lights get covered by the particles of debris that float in all ponds. To clean the lenses without removing the lights from the water, simply direct a gentle hose over them.

You will find that occasionally you have to remove a light and wash the lens thoroughly in warm soapy water. Always disconnect the power supply before you handle the lights or take them out of the pond.

Run the flex for pool lighting under the edging stones via a drain made from corrugated plastic sheeting. The entire length of the flex can be protected from adverse weather by being run through a

length of ordinary garden hose. Take the safest route to the power supply, anchoring the flex gently in convenient spots – but don't cover it with grass or soil in a place where someone might inadvertently cut through the flex with a spade or fork. Join lengths of low-voltage cable with waterproof connectors.

Floating pond lights illuminate this fountain

Pumps

Electric pumps can be used in garden pools to create fountains and waterfalls. A combination unit will send an adjustable jet of water up into the air and at the same time pump water through a plastic tube to the top of a rockery to trickle back into the pool.

Some pumps run directly from the mains supply, but there are also extra-low-voltage pumps that connect to a transformer (see left) shielded from the weather. So you can disconnect the pump without disturbing the extra-low-voltage wiring to the transformer, join two lengths of cable with a waterproof connector. Conceal the connector under a stone or gravel beside the pool.

Most manufacturers recommend you take a pump from the water at the end of each season and clean it thoroughly, then return it to the water immediately. To avoid corrosion, don't leave it out of the water for very long without cleaning and drying it. Never service a pump without first disconnecting it from the power supply. During the winter, run the pump for at least an hour every week, to keep it in good working order.

• **Connected kits**
You do not have to notify your Building Control Officer if you are installing a complete ready-connected lighting kit or pump that is CE approved and that is not part of the fixed wiring of the house.

• **'Extra-low-voltage'**
Strictly speaking, this is the correct term to describe equipment that runs on 50V or less. However, suppliers and manufacturers often use the term 'low-voltage' to describe equipment of this kind.

Waterproof cable connector
You can obtain suitable cable connectors from pump and lighting suppliers.

Beautifully constructed miniature waterfall

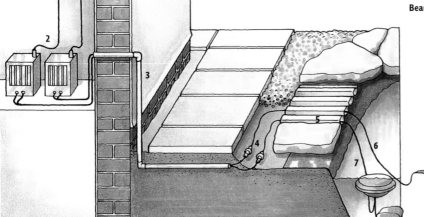

Low-voltage pump and lighting circuits
1 Socket outlet
2 Isolating transformers BS 3535 Type 3 (also numbered BS EN 60742).
3 Plastic conduit
4 Waterproof connectors
5 Home-made drain
6 Pump cable
7 Lighting cable

SEE ALSO > Building Regulations 8

Running power to outbuildings

The power supply to a separate workshop, garage or tool shed can't be tapped from other domestic circuits. The cable has to run either from from its own fuseway in the consumer unit or a separate switchfuse unit, and pass safely underground or overhead to the outside location – where it can be wired into a switchfuse unit from which the various circuits in the outbuilding can be distributed as required.

Types of cable permitted outdoors

Three types of cable can be used outside. The type you choose will depend on how you wish to run the cable.

N If you undertake work marked with this symbol, you must inform the BCO before starting – see FIRST THINGS FIRST.

Armoured
Although insulated in the ordinary way, this two-core or three-core cable has additional protection in the form of steel-wire armour. There is also an outer sheath of PVC. With two-core cable, the metal armour provides the path to earth, but as some authorities insist on two-core-and-earth cable, check what is required before you buy your cable.

Armoured cable is expensive and has to be terminated at a special junction box at each end of its run, where it can be joined to ordinary PVC-insulated cable. It is fitted with threaded glands for attaching it to the junction boxes. When buried in the ground, this type of cable must be covered with cable covers or warning tape.

Mineral-insulated copper-sheathed
The bare copper conductors of mineral-insulated copper-sheathed (MICS) cable are tightly packed in magnesium-oxide powder

within a copper sheathing. The copper sheathing can act as the earth conductor. Because the mineral powder absorbs moisture, special seals must be fitted at the ends of the cable.

Like armoured cable, MICS cable is costly and has to be terminated at special junction boxes so that cheaper cable can be used in the outbuilding itself. It must also be protected with cable covers or warning tape when it is buried below ground.

PVC-insulated-and-sheathed
Ordinary PVC-insulated two-core-and-earth cable can be run underground to an outbuilding – but only if it is protected with impact-resistant heavy-gauge conduit and paving slabs that will, together, provide at least the same degree of mechanical protection as armoured cable.

If the conduit has to go round corners, elbow joints can be cemented onto the ends of straight sections. The cable itself should be continuous.

PVC-insulated cable can also be run overhead quite safely – but only under certain specified conditions (see below).

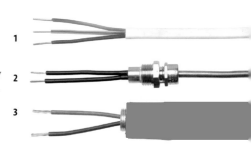

Outdoor cables
1 PVC-insulated-and-sheathed cable
2 Mineral-insulated copper-sheathed cable
3 Armoured cable

Ways of running outdoor cable

Underground
Running cable underground is usually the best way of supplying electricity to an outbuilding. You should bury the cable in a trench at least 500mm (1ft 8in) deep, or deeper still if the cable has to pass underneath a vegetable plot or flowerbed, or other areas where digging is likely to go on. It's best to plan the cable run so as to avoid such areas where possible. But extra protection can be provided for the cable by laying housebricks along both sides of it, supporting a covering of paving slabs. Line the bottom of the trench with finely sifted soil or sand.

Special black-and-yellow-striped tape should be buried above the cable to serve as a warning to anyone who happens to uncover the slabs at a later date.

Overhead
Ordinary PVC-insulated cable can be run from house to outbuilding provided it is at least 3.5m (12ft) above the ground or 5.2m (17ft) above a driveway that's accessible to vehicles. The cable may not be used unsupported over a distance of more than 3m (10ft), though the same distance can be spanned by running the cable through a continuous length of rigid steel conduit suspended at a height of at least 3m (10ft) above the ground or 5.2m (17ft) above a driveway. The conduit must be earthed.

Over greater distances, the cable must be supported by a taut metal catenary wire, which must be earthed. The cable needs to be clipped to it or hung from slings.

PVC-insulated cable can also be run through conduit mounted on a wall.

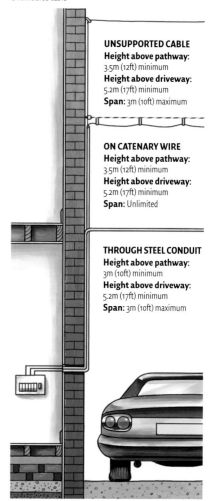

UNSUPPORTED CABLE
Height above pathway:
3.5m (12ft) minimum
Height above driveway:
5.2m (17ft) minimum
Span: 3m (10ft) maximum

ON CATENARY WIRE
Height above pathway:
3.5m (12ft) minimum
Height above driveway:
5.2m (17ft) minimum
Span: Unlimited

THROUGH STEEL CONDUIT
Height above pathway:
3m (10ft) minimum
Height above driveway:
5.2m (17ft) minimum
Span: 3m (10ft) maximum

Running cable overhead

SEE ALSO > Building Regulations 8, Cables 26

Running the circuit   N

There are various ways to run a circuit to a workshop or other outbuilding. The method described here suggests using PVC-insulated cable run from a fuseway in the consumer unit to a switchfuse unit in the outbuilding. If there's no spare fuseway in your consumer unit, the outgoing cable can run from a separate switchfuse unit – but the wiring is complicated by having to connect the unit to the meter, so is probably best left to a professional.

The cable is shown running underground in heavy-gauge plastic conduit protected by paving slabs. It must enter both buildings above the DPC. It's assumed here that both sockets and lighting are required in the outbuilding, so the lighting circuit is taken from the power cable via a junction box and an unswitched fused connection unit.

House end of the circuit

Ideally, the outgoing 4mm² two-core-and-earth cable should run from a 32amp MCB or 30amp circuit fuse in the consumer unit. In addition, the circuit must be protected by an RCD.

Alternative arrangement

If there's no room for the new circuit in your consumer unit, mount a 30amp switchfuse unit containing a 30amp circuit fuse near the meter (see right). A separate residual current device must be installed between the unit and the meter. Use a 10mm² two-core-and-earth cable to connect the RCD to the 'Mains' terminals of the switchfuse unit. Connect the outgoing 4mm² to the 'Load' terminals of the switchfuse unit.

Connect a pair of 16mm² meter leads – one brown and one blue – to the 'Mains' terminals of the residual current device. Wire a 16mm² earth lead to the RCD in readiness for connection to the consumer's earth terminal.

After the BCO has made the necessary tests, the electricity company will make the connections to the meter and the company's earth.

Outbuilding end of circuit

Run 4mm² two-core-and-earth cable through conduit from the house to the outbuilding, terminating at a 30amp switchfuse unit mounted on the wall.

Connect the incoming cable to the supply or 'Mains' terminals of the switchfuse unit, and run an outgoing 4mm² cable from its 'Load' terminals to the outbuilding's sockets (1).

Insert a 30amp junction box at some point along the power cable (2), and run a 4mm² spur from it to an unswitched fused connection unit fitted with a 3amp fuse. Run a 1.5mm² two-core-and-earth cable from the connection unit to the light fitting and switch.

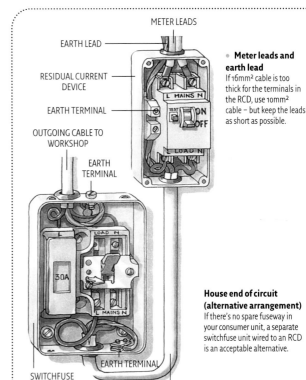

Meter leads and earth lead
If 16mm² cable is too thick for the terminals in the RCD, use 10mm² cable – but keep the leads as short as possible.

METER LEADS
EARTH LEAD
RESIDUAL CURRENT DEVICE
EARTH TERMINAL
OUTGOING CABLE TO WORKSHOP
EARTH TERMINAL
30A
SWITCHFUSE UNIT
EARTH TERMINAL
10mm² CABLE

House end of circuit (alternative arrangement)
If there's no spare fuseway in your consumer unit, a separate switchfuse unit wired to an RCD is an acceptable alternative.

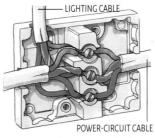

WORKSHOP CIRCUIT CABLE
EARTH TERMINAL
30A
EARTH TERMINAL
CABLE FROM HOUSE

1 Wiring workshop switchfuse unit

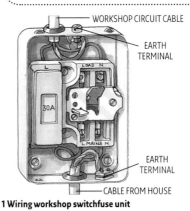

LIGHTING CABLE
POWER-CIRCUIT CABLE

2 Wiring junction box on power circuit

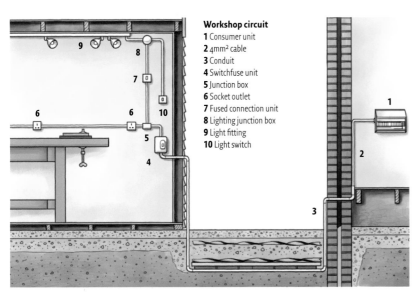

Workshop circuit
1 Consumer unit
2 4mm² cable
3 Conduit
4 Switchfuse unit
5 Junction box
6 Socket outlet
7 Fused connection unit
8 Lighting junction box
9 Light fitting
10 Light switch

SEE ALSO > Building Regulations 8, Testing circuits 12–13, Switching off 20, Running cables 27–9, Connecting sockets 32, Fused connection units 34, Lighting circuits 48, Fitting track lighting 52, One way-switch 44, New switch and light 55

Complete wiring Ⓝ

When you are working on a single circuit the rest of the household can function normally, but to renew all the circuits means that every part of your home will eventually be affected. Few of us would contemplate taking on such a time-consuming task. And even if you do feel competent to undertake extensive rewiring, the additional burden of obtaining and paying for formal testing and certification might make you think again.

Ⓝ If you undertake work marked with this symbol, you must inform the BCO before starting – see FIRST THINGS FIRST.

A full-time professional will be able to cope with every aspect of the job in such a way that inconvenience is kept to a minimum. So unless you are able to make the wiring a full-time commitment for at least a week or two, you would be well advised to employ an electrician who can undertake the work and deal with the paperwork on your behalf.

Perhaps he or she may allow you to work alongside – which could mean a saving on the cost if you are able to carry out some of the more mundane tasks, such as running cable under floorboards and channelling out plaster and brickwork.

Circuits: maximum lengths

The maximum length of a circuit is limited by the permitted voltage drop and the time it takes to operate the fuse or MCB in the event of an earth fault.

The method for calculation given in the Wiring Regulations is extremely complicated – but the table below will provide you with a simple method for determining the maximum cable lengths for common domestic circuits.

If necessary, plan to split up your circuits so that none of the indicated cable lengths are exceeded. If your requirements fall outside the limits of this chart, ask a professional electrician to make the calculations for you.

Rewirable fuses are not included, as they are subject to special restrictions – which makes them an unwise choice.

Most two-core-and-earth cables have a standard-size protective circuit conductor (earth wire). In each case, the chart below shows the size of earth wire used in the calculations.

The maximum circuit lengths given in the chart are based on the assumption that you won't install any electrical cables where the ambient temperature exceeds 30°C (86°F), that no cables will be bunched together, and that you will not cover any of the cables with thermal insulation.

The shower-circuit lengths assume that a 30 milliamp residual current device is used in the circuit.

The cooker-circuit lengths allow for using a cooker control unit with a built-in socket outlet. However, you can safely use the same figures for wiring a control unit without a built-in socket.

Designing your system

Before you set up a meeting with a professional, you need to form clear ideas about the kind of installation you want. A proper specification should enable you to avoid expensive modifications.

Choosing the best consumer unit
It is worth installing the best consumer unit you can afford. Choose one that has MCBs or cartridge fuses. and make sure it has enough spare fuseways for possible additional circuits.

Ask the electrician about the advantages of installing a split consumer unit, with a residual current device (RCD) protecting only the most vulnerable circuits

Power circuits
Ring circuits are better than radial circuits for supplying socket outlets. Provided that the floor area in question does not exceed 100sq m (120sq yds), you can have as many sockets as you want. Economizing on the cost of a few sockets now could cause you considerable inconvenience in the future – for example, there's little point in opting for a single socket outlet when you can fit a double for about the same price.

Lighting circuits
Modern domestic lighting is normally designed around a loop-in system; but you can supply individual lights from junction boxes if that is the most practical solution.

You should insist on a lighting circuit for each floor – so that you will never be left totally without electric lights if a fuse should blow. In the interests of safety, make sure you have two-way or three-way switches installed for lights in passageways and on landings and staircases.

Additional circuits
Decide what additional circuits you are going to need – such as a radial circuit for an immersion heater or for a hob-and-oven combination. Are you going to want lighting outdoors, or other exterior wiring? Now's the time to incorporate the work, rather than call in another electrician later.

TYPE OF CIRCUIT	Max. floor area in m²	Cable size in mm²	Size of earth wire in mm²	USING FUSES		USING MCBs	
				Current rating of circuit fuse	Max cable length using cartridge fuse	Current rating of MCB	Max cable length using MCB
RING CIRCUIT	100	2.5	1.5	30amp	65	32amp	65
RADIAL CIRCUIT	20	2.5	1.5	15amp	60	20amp	60
COOKER up to 13.5kW with socket outlet		6	2.5	30amp	42	32amp	42
COOKER from 13.5 to 18kW		6	2.5	45amp	32	40amp	32
IMMERSION HEATER		2.5	1.5	15amp	39	16amp	39
SHOWER up to 9.2kW		10	4	45amp	31	40amp	52
SHOWER from 9.2 to 11.4kW		10	4		N/A	50amp	25
STORAGE HEATER up to 3.375kW		2.5	1.5	15amp	35	16amp	35
FIXED LIGHTING including switch drops		1.5	1	5amp	100	6amp	100

MAXIMUM LENGTHS FOR DOMESTIC CIRCUITS

Note: Longer lengths may be permissible with detailed calculations, which will require system information from your supplier.

SEE ALSO > Building Regulations 8, Consumer units 22, Fuses and MCBs 23, Domestic circuits 25

Electrical tools

You need only a limited range of tools to make electrical connections, but an extensive general-purpose tool kit is required for making cable runs and mounting electrical accessories.

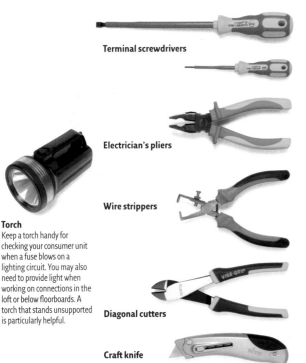

Terminal screwdrivers

Electrician's pliers

Wire strippers

Diagonal cutters

Craft knife

Torch
Keep a torch handy for checking your consumer unit when a fuse blows on a lighting circuit. You may also need to provide light when working on connections in the loft or below floorboards. A torch that stands unsupported is particularly helpful.

Terminal screwdrivers

A terminal screwdriver has a long, slim cylindrical shaft that is ground to a flat tip.

For turning screw terminals in sockets and larger appliances, buy a screwdriver with a plastic handle and a plastic insulating sleeve on its shaft. Use a smaller screwdriver with a very slim shaft to work on ceiling roses or to tighten plastic terminal blocks in small fittings.

Buy only good-quality screwdrivers – the soft tips on cheap ones soon twist out of shape.

Electrician's pliers

These are engineer's pliers with insulating sleeves shrunk onto their handles. You can use pliers to crop circuit conductors.

Diagonal cutters

Diagonal cutters will crop thick conductors more effectively than electrician's pliers, but you may need a junior hacksaw to cut meter leads.

Wire strippers

To remove the insulation from cable and flex, use a pair of wire strippers with jaws shaped to cut through the covering without damaging the wire core. There is a multi-purpose version that can both strip the insulation and crop conductors to length.

Craft knife

A knife with sharp disposable blades is best for slitting and peeling the sheathing encasing cable and flex.

Power drill

A cordless power drill is ideal for boring cable holes through timbers and for making wallplug fixings. As well as standard masonry bits for wall fixings, you will need a much longer bit for boring through brick walls and clearing access channels behind skirting boards.

If you shorten the shaft of a wide-tipped spade bit, you can use it in a power drill between floor joists.

Testers

You can buy reliable testers without having to spend a great deal of money. Most good DIY outlets stock a range of them.

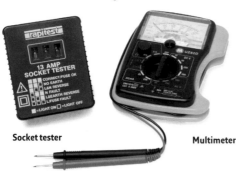

Socket tester

Multimeter

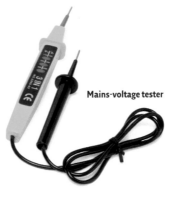

Mains-voltage tester

Mains-voltage tester

Mains testers are designed to tell you whether a circuit is completely 'dead' after you have turned off the power at the consumer unit. Be sure to buy a tester that's intended for use with mains voltage – similar devices are sold in auto shops for testing 12V car wiring only.

Multimeter

An electrician needs a multimeter, for measuring insulation resistance and continuity. There are digital instruments that give readings on an LCD screen, and there are analogue ones with a needle that moves across a scale on a dial. With some meters, you can select an audible signal to tell you when there is continuity.

Socket tester

A simple plug-in device can be used to test the connections inside a 13amp socket outlet without having to turn off the power or expose internal wiring.

General-purpose tools

Every electrician needs tools for lifting floorboards, cutting cables and fitting mounting boxes.

- Claw hammer – for nailing cable clips to walls and timbers.

- Club hammer and cold chisel – for cutting channels in plaster and brickwork in order to bury cables or mounting boxes.

- Cabinet screwdriver – for fixing mounting boxes to walls.

- Spirit level – for checking that mounting boxes are fixed horizontally.

- Plasterer's trowel or filling knife – for covering concealed cable with plaster or other kinds of filler.

- Bolster chisel – for levering up floorboards.

- Wood chisels – for notching floor joists.

- Padsaw or power jigsaw – for cutting through floorboards close to skirtings.

- A floorboard saw is the best tool for cutting through tongued and grooved floorboards.

- A small spanner is needed for making some earth connections.

SEE ALSO > Building Regulations 8, Testing 12–13

Glossary

ACCESSORY
An electrical component permanently connected to a circuit – a switch, socket outlet, fused connection unit etc.

ADAPTOR
A device that is used to connect more than one appliance to a socket outlet.

AMPERE (AMP/A)
A unit of measurement of the flow of electric current necessary to produce the required wattage for an appliance.

APPLIANCE
A machine or device powered by electricity. *or* A functional piece of equipment connected to the plumbing, such as a basin, sink, bath etc.

CEILING ROSE
A special junction box for connecting a suspended light fitting to a lighting circuit.

CEILING SWITCH
A light switch that is attached to a ceiling and operated by a pull-cord.

CHASE
A groove cut in masonry or plaster to accept pipework or an electrical cable. *or* To cut or channel such grooves.

CIRCUIT
A complete path through which an electric current can flow.

CIRCUIT BREAKER
A special switch installed in a consumer unit o protect an individual circuit. Should a fault occur, the circuit breaker will switch off automatically.

CONDUCTOR
A component, usually a length of wire, along which an electric current will pass.

CONSUMER UNIT
A box, situated near the meter, which contains the fuses of MCB's protecting all the circuits. It also houses the main isolating switch that cuts the power to the whole building.

DOUBLE-POLE SWITCH
A switch that breaks both the live and neutral conductors.

DOWNLIGHTER
A type of ceiling-mounted light fitting that directs a relatively narrow beam of light to the floor.

EARTH
A connection between an electrical circuit and the earth (ground). *or* A

terminal to which the connection is made.

EXTENSION LEAD
A length of electrical flex for temporarily connecting the short permanent flex of an appliance to a wall socket.

FUSE
A protective device containing a thin wire that is designed to melt at a given temperature caused by an excess flow of current on a circuit.

FUSE BOARD
Where the main electrical service cable is connected to the house circuitry. *or* The accumulation of consumer unit, meter etc.

GROMMET
A ring of rubber or plastic used to line a hole to protect electrical cable from chafing. A blind grommet incorporates a thin web of plastic or rubber that seals the hole until the web is cut to provide access for a cable.

IMMERSION HEATER
An electrical element designed to heat water in a storage cylinder.

INSULATION – ELECTRICAL
Nonconductive material surrounding electrical wires or connections to prevent the passage of electricity.

INSULATION – THERMAL
Materials used to reduce the transmission of heat.

MINIATURE CIRCUIT BREAKER (MCB)
See Circuit breaker.

NEUTRAL
The section of an electrical circuit that carries the flow of current back to source.

NOGGING
A short horizontal wooden member between studs.

PHASE
The part of an electrical circuit that carries the flow of current to an appliance or accessory. Also known as live.

PROTECTIVE MULTIPLE EARTH (PME)
A system of electrical wiring in which the neutral part of the circuit is used to take earth-leakage current to earth.

RADIAL CIRCUIT
A power cicuit feeding a number of socket outlets or fused connection units and terminating at the last accessory.

RESIDUAL CURRENT DEVICE (RCD)
A device that monitors the flow of electrical current through the live and neutral wires of a circuit. When an RCD detects an imbalance caused by earth leakage, it cuts off the supply of electricity as a safety precaution.

RING CIRCUIT
A continuous power circuit starting at and returning to the consumer unit. Also known as ring main.

SHEATHING
The outer layer of insulation surrounding an electrical cable or flex.

SHORT CIRCUIT
The accidental rerouting of electricity to earth, which increases the flow of current and blows a fuse.

SPUR
A short length of cable that feeds a socket outlet or fused connection unit by taking its power via another similar accessory.

STUDS
The vertical members of a timber-frame wall.

SUPPLEMENTARY BONDING
The connecting to earth of electrical appliances and exposed metal pipework in a bathroom or kitchen.

TERMINAL
A connection to which the bared ends of electrical cable or flex are attached.

TRANSFORMER
A device that increases or decreases the voltage on an electrical circuit.

VOLT
A unit of measurement of 'pressure' that is provided by Electricity Company generators and which drives the current along the conductors

Index